food + drink

acknowledgments

A big thank you to Kay Scarlett for having faith, Anna Waddington for all her assistance and Jackie Frank for giving me the opportunity to do this book. Thanks also to Susan Gray and David Herbert for all their hard work in the face of editorial adversity, and to Michelle Cutler for her art direction.

My studio team were a dream. A big hug to Ross Dobson for all his wonderful food and good humour, and another to Cathy Armstrong for her assistance throughout the long process of bringing this book to fruition. Apologies also to Geoff Lung for taking over his studio and laughing too much. And last but by no means least, thank you to Petrina Tinslay for her beautiful photography and guidance. This book would not have been possible without you.

This list wouldn't be complete without thanking the '97 – '98 kitchen team at Urban Productions in London, where many of these recipes first appeared.

Thanks also to Tyler, Neale, Victoria, Joanna and Ken. And to the best mum and dad, a big thank you for all your support and friendship.

Many thanks to Orson & Blake, Empire Homewares and The Bay Tree for their beautiful homewares. Thank you also to Mud Australia for their beautiful matt plates and bowls, and David Edmonds for his inspiring ceramics.

Published by Murdoch Books®, a division of Murdoch Magazines Pty Ltd.

AUSTRALIA:
Murdoch Books® Australia
GPO Box 1203
Sydney NSW 2001
Phone: (612) 8220 2000
Fax: (612) 8220 2558

UK:
Murdoch Books® UK
Ferry House
51–57 Lacy Road
London SW15 1PR
Phone: (020) 8355 1480
Fax: (020) 8355 1499

Author and Stylist: Michele Cranston
Photographer: Petrina Tinslay
Designer: Michelle Culter
Project Manager: Anna Waddington
Editor: Susan Gray
Food Editor: David Herbert
Food Preparation: Ross Dobson

Publisher: Kay Scarlett
Group General Manager: Mark Smith
Production Manager: Liz Fitzgerald
Creative Director: Marylouise Brammer

National Library of Australia Cataloguing-in-Publication Data
Cranston, Michele.
Food and drink.
Includes index.
ISBN 1 74045 092 2.
1. Cookery. 2. Entertaining. I. Tinslay, Petrina. II. Title. III. Title: Marie Claire.
641.568

Text © Michele Cranston 2001. Photography © Petrina Tinslay 2001. Design © Murdoch Books® 2001.
Printed by Toppan Printing Hong Kong Co. Ltd. PRINTED IN CHINA. First printed 2001.

marie claire

food + drink

michele cranston

photography by
petrina tinslay

MURDOCH
BOOKS

contents

With our busy lives, entertaining these days tends to be about gathering friends together at whatever time is available, whether it is a simple breakfast of spiced fruit and rhubarb smoothies, a casual lunch of chilli quesadillas and rose petal sherbet, a stylish afternoon tea of cucumber sandwiches, a return to the cocktail hour with gin fizzes and duck pancakes, or after-dark treats of liqueur and ice cream shots.

marie claire food + drink is about those occasions, whether formal or relaxed. From breakfast fruit whips and tasty, light snacks through to late-night drinks and luscious desserts, this is a book full of easy-to-follow recipes, most of which can be served as small grazing portions or as conventional meals. These simple food and drink recipes are accompanied with quick and stylish ideas which will make dinner for six or a party for 100 a breeze. Continuing in the *marie claire* tradition, this book will inspire with its modern, fresh approach to food and entertaining.

More information about ingredients and recipes marked with a star* can be found in the glossary.

morning

breakfast

More than any other meal of the day, breakfast should be about starting with high-quality ingredients. Since a great breakfast can be as simple as fresh fruit juice and nutty toast, indulge in the best.

great coffee

The world can be divided between those who prefer coffee and those who prefer tea first thing in the morning. For many, a coffee kick-start is one of life's little essentials. For good coffee, use fresh beans stored in an airtight container and grind them as you need them. If buying ground coffee, ensure that the grind suits your coffee maker, be it plunger, percolator or espresso machine.

a favourite tea

While coffee is a great way to start the day, a pot of leaf tea manages to be both comforting and refreshing. As with coffee, there is a ritual to making a good cup of tea. Always heat the pot beforehand and add freshly boiled water to your favourite tea blend. Allow it to steep for approximately the same length of time as it takes to toast a slice of bread, and enjoy more than one cup.

yoghurt

Whenever possible, buy organic natural yoghurt or, at the very least, a yoghurt with a live culture. The culture present in yoghurt is believed to aid digestion, so eat up secure in the knowledge that you're doing yourself a favour. Enjoy adding your own flavourings, like fresh fruit, honey, vanilla, maple syrup, citrus zest or, for the ultimate indulgence, finely grated white chocolate.

bread and butter

The flavour difference between toasted commercial white bread spread with margarine, and a hearty doorstop of sourdough or mixed-grain bread oozing with cultured butter, says it all. Always buy fresh, good-quality butter, and head to the local bakery for your bread. Treating friends and family doesn't come much easier than with great bread, home-made jam and a pot of coffee, so why settle for less?

blend it

There is no better way to start the day than with a fresh juice or smoothie. On weekends, lay all the essential ingredients along the benchtop and invite your friends to create their own combinations.

blend it

yoghurt

bread and butter

great coffee

a favourite tea

good ideas

flavoured butters

Butter can be flavoured with just about anything, from fresh herbs, roasted tomato, caramelised onion, roasted garlic, vanilla, honey, citrus zest, preserved ginger or lemon, toasted spices, roasted nuts or confectionery honeycomb.

flavoured syrups

If pancakes and waffles are a favourite breakfast item, invest in a bottle of real maple syrup, or make your own flavoured syrups by adding vanilla, citrus or fresh fruit purée to a simple sugar syrup*.

boiled eggs

Zest up the morning egg with a selection of great accompaniments like sweet chilli sauce, roughly chopped fresh herbs, diced avocado, smoked salmon, spiced salt, pitted olives, fresh tomatoes and ground black pepper.

honeyed nuts

Spruce up yoghurt with a sprinkling of honeyed nuts. In a small pan, warm 2 tablespoons of honey and a teaspoon of butter. Add half a cup each of almonds, pine nuts, sunflower seeds and sesame seeds, and stir over low heat until well coated. Remove from the heat and squeeze over a little lemon juice.

smoked fish

Pep up a breakfast with the addition of smoked fish. Smoked salmon can be teamed with peppery avocado toast or piled on brioche, while flaked smoked ocean trout tossed with parsley and a sliced boiled egg is an easy brunch solution.

frozen fruit pulp

When berries, mangoes or passionfruit are in season, think ahead and save the pulped fruit as frozen ice cubes. They are a great addition to any blended fruit drink, or can be defrosted and simmered with a little sugar to bring the taste of summer to your morning bowl of yoghurt.

bacon twists

Nothing heralds the call to breakfast more than the smell of grilled bacon. Make twists of bacon by winding rashers around skewers and grilling or baking until crisp and brown.

EGG FLIP In a blender, place 1 cup (8 fl oz) of milk, 1 tablespoon of natural yoghurt, 1 fresh organic egg and 1 tablespoon of honey. Blend until the honey has dissolved, then pour into a chilled glass. Drink immediately. Serves 1.

BANANA AND HONEY SMOOTHIE In a blender, place 1 roughly chopped banana, 3/4 cup (6 fl oz) of natural yoghurt, 1 tablespoon of honey, a generous pinch of nutmeg and 8 ice cubes. Blend until smooth and serve immediately. Serves 2.

HONEYDEW AND PINEAPPLE WHIP In a blender, place 1 cup (8 fl oz) of fresh pineapple juice, 1 cup of chopped honeydew melon, 1 tablespoon of lime juice and 6 ice cubes. Blend until smooth and pour into glasses. Serves 2.

SUMMER MORNING In a blender, combine half a banana, 1 cup of chopped fresh pineapple, the pulp of 2 passionfruit, 6 large mint leaves and 8 ice cubes. Blend to a smooth consistency and serve immediately in chilled glasses. Serves 2.

peach waffles

breakfast trifles

citrus compote

peach waffles

½ cup sugar
½ vanilla bean, split and scraped
juice of 1 lemon
2 large freestone peaches, peeled
   and cut into eighths
1 quantity waffles*

Place 400 ml (13 fl oz) of water, the sugar, vanilla and
lemon juice in a saucepan and bring to the boil, stirring
to dissolve the sugar. Add the peach segments and
return to the boil. Reduce the heat and simmer gently
for 2 minutes. Place the fruit in a bowl and reduce the
liquid over medium heat for 10–15 minutes to produce
a thick syrup. Pour over the peaches.
Cook the waffles in a lightly greased waffle iron until
golden. Serve a waffle segment topped with a piece
of peach and drizzle with the syrup. Makes 16.

breakfast trifles

1½ cups (12 fl oz) honey-flavoured yoghurt
2 cups toasted muesli
2 cups fruit of choice — diced mangoes,
   peaches or mixed berries

Stir the yoghurt well until it is smooth and creamy.
Layer the muesli, yoghurt and fruit into small glasses,
finishing with fruit on top. Serve accompanied with
a tiny spoon. Makes 8 small glasses.

citrus compote

3 limes
3 oranges
2 pink grapefruits
1 vanilla bean, finely chopped
1 teaspoon sugar
1 cup (8 fl oz) honey-flavoured yoghurt

Zest 1 lime and 1 orange and place in a medium-sized
bowl. Peel the limes, oranges and grapefruits with a sharp
knife. Cut the flesh into segments, or thinly slice, saving
any juice. Add the vanilla bean, sugar and reserved juice
and mix to combine. Serve with honey yoghurt. Makes
8–10 small serves or 4 regular serves.

papaya and coconut sambal

2 teaspoons vegetable oil
1 small onion, finely diced
2 tablespoons finely sliced lemon grass,
   white part only
2 teaspoons sambal oelek*
½ cup desiccated coconut, toasted
2 teaspoons brown sugar
papaya, to serve

Heat the oil in a frying pan over medium heat and cook
the onion, lemon grass and sambal oelek for 5 minutes,
stirring occasionally. Reduce the heat to low and add
the coconut, ½ teaspoon of salt and the sugar and cook,
stirring regularly, for 12–15 minutes or until golden and
crisp. Remove from the heat and allow to cool.
Place the mixture in a food processor and process until
the mixture resembles breadcrumbs. To serve, slice the
papaya into thin wedges and sprinkle with the sambal.
note – Excess coconut sambal may be stored in an
airtight container until ready to use.

papaya and coconut sambal

LEMON CHEESECAKE DRINK Blend 1/2 cup (4 fl oz) of natural yoghurt, 1/4 cup (2 fl oz) of cream, 2 tablespoons of caster (superfine) sugar, 2 tablespoons of lemon juice, 1/2 teaspoon of vanilla essence and 1 cup of ice cubes. Pour into glasses and top with grated nutmeg. Serves 2.

BERRY SMOOTHIE In a blender, place 1/2 cup each of strawberries, blackberries and raspberries, 1/4 cup (2 fl oz) of sugar syrup*, 3 tablespoons of natural yoghurt and 6 ice cubes. Blend until smooth and pour into chilled glasses. Serves 2.

RHUBARB SMOOTHIE In a blender, combine 1 cup of cooled stewed rhubarb*, 1¹/₂ cups (12 fl oz) of natural yoghurt, ¹/₂ teaspoon of cinnamon and 16 ice cubes. Blend until smooth. Pour the mixture into chilled glasses and drink immediately. Serves 4.

FIG AND HONEY SMOOTHIE In a blender, place 2 ripe black figs (roughly chopped), 1 tablespoon of honey, ³/₄ cup (6 fl oz) of natural yoghurt and 8 ice cubes. Blend until smooth. Pour into glasses and lightly stir through 3 tablespoons of finely chopped walnuts. Serves 2.

scrambled egg tartlets

pumpkin muffins with marmalade   zucchini and marjoram frittatas

scrambled egg tartlets

2 slices prosciutto*, each sliced into 12 pieces
4 eggs
3/4 cup (6 fl oz) cream
30 g (1 oz) butter
24 pre-baked tart shells*

Preheat the oven to 180°C (350°F). Place the prosciutto on a baking tray lined with baking paper and grill or bake until crisp. Remove and drain on paper towels. Place the eggs and cream in a bowl and lightly whisk together. Season well with salt and pepper. Place half the butter in a non-stick frying pan over medium heat and add half the egg mixture. Slowly fold together. When just set, remove from the heat. Spoon the cooked mixture into half of the tart shells and top each tart with a piece of prosciutto. Grease the pan with the remaining butter and repeat the process with the leftover egg mixture. Serve immediately. Makes 24.

pumpkin muffins with marmalade

300 g (10 oz) pumpkin, peeled and cut into chunks
1 1/4 cups self-raising (self-rising) flour
1/2 teaspoon grated nutmeg
1/2 cup caster (superfine) sugar
1 large egg
2 tablespoons natural yoghurt
35 g (1 1/4 oz) butter, melted
1/3 cup pine nuts, toasted
extra butter, softened, to serve
bitter orange marmalade, to serve

Place the pumpkin in a saucepan of water and boil until tender. Drain and mash the pumpkin.
Preheat the oven to 180°C (350°F). Sift the flour, nutmeg and a pinch of salt into a large bowl, stir in the sugar and make a well in the centre of the mixture. In a separate bowl, beat together the egg, yoghurt, mashed pumpkin and melted butter and pour into the well in the flour mixture. Stir until just combined. Gently stir through the pine nuts and spoon into 36 greased mini patty tins (lined with paper patty cases if desired). Bake for 10–12 minutes, then cool on a wire rack. Slice in half, butter and spread with bitter orange marmalade. Makes 36.

zucchini and marjoram frittatas

20 g (3/4 oz) butter
1 red onion, finely sliced
1 teaspoon finely chopped fresh marjoram leaves
1 1/2 cups grated zucchini (courgette)
6 eggs
1/2 cup grated fresh parmesan cheese

Preheat the oven to 180°C (350°F). Heat the butter in a frying pan and sauté the onion and marjoram over medium heat for 7–10 minutes, or until the onion is soft and caramelised. Spoon the mixture into two lightly greased, deep, 12-holed patty cake tins and top with the grated zucchini. Whisk the eggs with a tablespoon of water and season with salt and ground white pepper. Fill each of the patty tins with the egg mixture and sprinkle with the parmesan. Bake for 10 minutes or until set. Makes 24.

eggy crêpe roll-up

sweet pepper filling
1 tablespoon olive oil
2 teaspoons ground cumin
1 teaspoon ground coriander
2 teaspoons mustard seeds
2 red onions, diced
2 cloves garlic, finely chopped
1 red capsicum (pepper), diced
1 yellow capsicum (pepper), diced
1 tablespoon balsamic vinegar
crêpes
1/3 cup finely sliced fresh chives
1 quantity crêpe mixture*
50 g (1 3/4 oz) butter, softened
1/2 cup finely chopped fresh coriander (cilantro) leaves

Heat the oil in a frying pan over high heat and add the cumin, coriander and the mustard seeds. When the mustard seeds begin to pop, add the onion and garlic. Reduce the heat and continue to cook for 5–7 minutes, stirring occasionally, until the onion is transparent. Add the capsicum, cover and cook for a further 15 minutes, stirring occasionally. Add the vinegar and season with salt and freshly ground black pepper.
Stir the chives through the crêpe batter. Grease a small frying pan with a little butter and place over medium heat. Add 2 tablespoons of batter and swirl the pan around until the mixture coats the surface. Cook for a few minutes until the edges are crisp, then turn and cook the other side for a further minute. Remove from the pan and repeat with the remaining batter. When all the crêpes are cooked, place a heaped tablespoon of the filling along the centre of each one, sprinkle with coriander and roll up. Makes 10.

eggy crêpe roll-up

mini danish

pineapple muffins

walnut cornbread with bacon

cheese and olive sandwiches

mini danish

1 sheet ready-prepared puff pastry
1 egg
1/4 cup (2 fl oz) milk
1 quantity pastry cream*
4 small plums, sliced into eighths

Preheat the oven to 180°C (350°F). Divide the sheet of pastry into 16 small squares. Beat the egg and milk together and set aside. Place each of the squares into a shallow patty cake tin, prick the bases with a fork and fill with a teaspoon of pastry cream. Top with sliced plums. Fold the pastry over the fruit to enclose it a little, then glaze with the egg wash. Bake for 12–15 minutes, or until golden brown. Serve warm or at room temperature. Makes 16.

walnut cornbread with bacon

1 tablespoon walnut oil
1 cup (8 fl oz) milk
90 g (3 oz) unsalted butter
5 rashers of bacon, finely sliced
   (approximately 200 g / 6½ oz)
1 cup polenta (cornmeal)
2½ cups plain (all-purpose) flour
2 teaspoons baking powder
1 teaspoon bicarbonate of soda (baking soda)
3 eggs
100 ml (3½ fl oz) yoghurt
3 spring (green) onions, finely sliced
2/3 cup coarsely chopped walnuts
extra butter, to serve

Preheat the oven to 180°C (350°F). Lightly grease two 12-hole mini muffin tins with walnut oil. Warm the milk and butter in a small saucepan. When the butter has melted, remove from the heat.
Place the bacon in a frying pan and cook until it has browned but is not crisp. Remove from the heat.
Sift the dry ingredients and 1/2 teaspoon of salt into a mixing bowl and make a well in the centre. Whisk the eggs with the yoghurt and warm milk and fold into the dry ingredients until just blended. Add the spring onions, walnuts and bacon and lightly fold through the batter. Spoon half the mixture into the greased tins (lined with paper patty cases if desired) and bake for 15–20 minutes, or until firm and golden. Repeat with the remaining mixture. Serve warm, spread with butter. Makes 48.

pineapple muffins

1 3/4 cups plain (all-purpose) flour
2 teaspoons baking powder
3/4 cup sugar
1/2 teaspoon cinnamon
1 1/4 cups desiccated coconut
45 g (1½ oz) unsalted butter, melted
3/4 cup (6 fl oz) milk
2 eggs
1 cup diced fresh pineapple

Preheat the oven to 180°C (350°F). Sift the flour, baking powder and a pinch of salt into a large mixing bowl. Add the sugar, cinnamon and coconut and stir to combine. Make a well in the centre of the mixture and add the melted butter, milk and eggs. Mix until just combined and then fold the pineapple through.
Grease a patty tray or small muffin tray (lined with paper patty cases if desired) and place a heaped tablespoon of the mixture into each of the holes. Bake for 15–17 minutes, or until golden brown. Makes 18.

cheese and olive sandwiches

1/3 cup seeded and finely sliced green olives
100 g (3½ oz) mozzarella cheese*, grated
30 g (1 oz) fresh parmesan cheese, grated
2 tablespoons roughly chopped fresh flat-leaf
   (Italian) parsley
8 slices white bread, crusts removed
2 tablespoons olive oil

Preheat the oven to 180°C (350°F). Place the olives, mozzarella, parmesan and parsley in a bowl and mix well to combine. Brush four slices of bread with half the olive oil and place them, oiled side down, on a greased baking tray. Divide the cheese mixture evenly among the four slices of bread and top with the remaining four slices. Brush the tops of the sandwiches with the remaining oil and place in the oven for 10 minutes, turning if necessary. Remove and slice each piece into three fingers. Makes 12.

banana pancakes

panettone fingers with rhubarb

cinnamon french toast

banana pancakes

1/2 cup grated palm sugar* or brown sugar
1 cup (8 fl oz) fresh pineapple juice
1 tablespoon lime juice
2 bananas
2 tablespoons caster (superfine) sugar
30 g (1 oz) unsalted butter
1 quantity pancake mixture*

Place the sugar and pineapple juice in a small saucepan over high heat and bring to the boil. Reduce the heat and simmer until the juice has reduced by half and formed a syrup. Remove from the heat and stir the lime juice through. Slice the banana thinly and toss the slices in caster sugar. Heat a little butter in a frying pan over medium heat. Add a tablespoon of the pancake mixture to the pan and allow to cook for 1 minute. Top with banana and cook until bubbles appear. Turn and cook the pancake for a further 2 minutes. Remove and keep in a warm place. Repeat with the remaining batter and banana, adding more butter to the pan as required. Serve with a drizzle of the pineapple syrup. Makes 12–15.

panettone fingers with rhubarb

6 stems rhubarb, trimmed
1/2 teaspoon grated fresh ginger
1 teaspoon finely chopped orange zest
1/3 cup (2 3/4 fl oz) orange juice
1/2 vanilla bean, split and scraped
1/4 cup brown sugar
15 g (1/2 oz) unsalted butter
12 fingers panettone*, cut into 2 cm x 12 cm
   (3/4 inch x 5 inch) lengths
icing (confectioners') sugar, to serve

Preheat the oven to 180°C (350°F). Cut each rhubarb stem into two 12 cm (5 inch) lengths. Place the ginger, orange zest, orange juice, vanilla bean, brown sugar and butter in a stainless steel baking tray and place in the oven for a minute or two until the butter has melted. Remove from the oven and stir to combine. Add the rhubarb and toss together so that the rhubarb is well coated in the sugary mix. Return to the oven for 10 minutes. Turn the rhubarb over and cook for a further 10 minutes. Allow to cool. Toast each of the panettone fingers until golden and place a strip of rhubarb along each of them. Drizzle with a little of the syrup, sprinkle with icing sugar and serve. Makes 12.

cinnamon french toast

5 slices thick-sliced white bread,
   crusts removed
1 egg
1 tablespoon sugar
1 teaspoon ground cinnamon
1/2 cup (4 fl oz) milk
butter, for frying
extra sugar, for sprinkling
155 ml (5 fl oz) natural yoghurt, to serve
fresh seasonal fruit, to serve
100 ml (3 1/2 fl oz) maple syrup, to serve
2 tablespoons finely chopped toasted
   pecans, to serve

Cut each slice of bread in half to make rectangles. Beat the egg, sugar and cinnamon in a bowl and then add the milk. Melt a tablespoon of butter in a frying pan over medium heat. Dip the bread into the sweet milk mixture, covering both sides. Sprinkle one side of each piece of bread with sugar and gently fry, sugar side down, for 3 minutes or until the undersides are golden. Sprinkle the tops with a little sugar and flip over. Cook until golden and serve with yoghurt, fresh fruit, maple syrup and a sprinkle of pecans. Serves 5.

rosewater fruit salad

70 g (2 1/4 oz) dried figs
70 g (2 1/4 oz) dried apricots
70 g (2 1/4 oz) pitted prunes
1/4 cup sugar
1/4 cup (2 fl oz) orange juice
1 cinnamon stick
2 star anise
1/2 teaspoon rosewater*
1 cup (8 fl oz) natural yoghurt, to serve
1 cup flaked toasted almonds, to serve

Cut the dried fruit into bite-sized pieces and place in a small bowl. Place the sugar, 1 cup (8 fl oz) of water, the orange juice, cinnamon and star anise in a small saucepan and bring to the boil over moderate heat, stirring to dissolve the sugar. Boil gently for 5–6 minutes until a light syrup forms. Remove from the heat and stir the rosewater through. Pour the liquid over the prepared dried fruit and allow to soak for several hours, or preferably overnight. Serve accompanied with yoghurt and sprinkled with the flaked almonds. Serves 6.

rosewater fruit salad

pear and honey smoothie

mango, strawberry and apricot chiller

rockmelon and ginger whip   tamarind and peach cooler

pear and honey smoothie

2 Bartlett pears, or other green-skinned pears
1 tablespoon honey
1/2 cup (4 fl oz) natural yoghurt
8 ice cubes

Place all the ingredients in a blender with 1/2 cup (4 fl oz) of water and blend until smooth. Pour into tall glasses. Serves 2.

mango, strawberry and apricot chiller

1 mango, peeled, flesh removed
1 cup (8 fl oz) apricot nectar
6 strawberries
6 ice cubes

Place all the ingredients in a blender and blend until smooth. Pour into tall glasses. Serves 2.

rockmelon and ginger whip

1 tablespoon chopped fresh ginger
2 cups chopped ripe rockmelon (cantaloupe)
1/2 cup (4 fl oz) orange juice
8 ice cubes

Place all the ingredients in a blender and blend until smooth. Pour into tall glasses. Serves 2.

tamarind and peach cooler

1 cup (8 fl oz) tamarind water*
2 ripe peaches, peeled, halved and stoned
6–8 ice cubes

Place all the ingredients in a blender and blend until smooth. Taste and add a little sugar if desired. Pour into tall glasses. Serves 2.

bloody mary

150 g (5 oz) tomatoes, finely chopped
1/3 cup (2 3/4 fl oz) tomato juice
1/4 cup (2 fl oz) vodka
1/4 teaspoon Worcestershire sauce
1/4 teaspoon Tabasco sauce
1 teaspoon horseradish cream
1 teaspoon lime juice
ice, to serve
celery and freshly ground black pepper,
   to garnish

Place the diced tomato and 1/4 teaspoon of salt in a bowl and allow to sit for half an hour. Place the tomato pieces in a blender with the tomato juice and blend until smooth. Place the tomato juice into a shaker with the vodka, Worcestershire sauce, Tabasco sauce, horseradish cream and lime juice and shake vigorously. Pour over ice and garnish with a celery stick and some freshly ground black pepper. Serves 1.

bloody mary

potato latkes with smoked salmon

stuffed mushrooms   salmon and chive fritters

potato latkes with smoked salmon

45 g (1¹/₂ oz) butter
2 leeks, finely chopped
2 tablespoons fresh thyme leaves
2¹/₂ cups peeled and grated potato
2 eggs, lightly beaten
¹/₃ cup plain (all-purpose) flour
vegetable oil, for cooking
150 g (5 oz) smoked salmon

Heat the butter in a small saucepan, add the leeks and thyme and cook over low heat for 15–20 minutes, stirring occasionally, until the leeks are soft and slightly caramelised. Set aside to cool.

Mix together the grated potato, eggs and flour and season well with salt and freshly ground black pepper. Place the mixture into a sieve over a bowl and press down to remove excess moisture. Add enough vegetable oil to a frying pan to cover the base by 5 mm (¹/₄ inch). Heat the oil over medium heat and add heaped teaspoons of the potato mixture. Flatten a little and cook each side for 4–5 minutes or until golden, and drain on paper towels. Repeat until all the mixture has been cooked.

To assemble, cut the salmon into 45 x 5 mm (¹/₄ inch) lengths. Place a slice of salmon on each latke and top with a small amount of leek. Makes 45.

stuffed mushrooms

¹/₄ cup ricotta cheese
¹/₂ teaspoon finely chopped fresh marjoram
¹/₄ teaspoon finely chopped fresh rosemary
2 slices prosciutto*, finely sliced
2 teaspoons virgin olive oil
18 button mushrooms

Preheat the oven to 180°C (350°F). Place the ricotta, herbs, prosciutto and oil in a small bowl and stir to combine. Season well with salt and freshly ground black pepper. Remove the stems from the mushrooms and trim their rounded tops with a sharp knife so as to give them a flat base when placed upside down. Spoon the ricotta filling into the centre of the mushrooms and place them on a baking tray. Lightly season with salt and pepper and bake for 12–15 minutes. Makes 18.

salmon and chive fritters

250 g (8 oz) salmon fillet, boned and skin removed
3 teaspoons finely chopped lemon zest
2 eggs, lightly beaten
1 cup plain (all-purpose) flour
1 teaspoon baking powder
2 tablespoons natural yoghurt
¹/₂ cup finely sliced garlic chives
1 cup finely sliced spring (green) onions
vegetable oil, for cooking
lemon wedges, to serve

Slice the salmon to form 1 cm (¹/₂ inch) dice. Place in a small bowl, cover and refrigerate until ready to use. Place the zest, eggs, flour, baking powder and yoghurt in a bowl and whisk until smooth. Just prior to cooking, fold the salmon, garlic chives and spring onions through the batter until evenly mixed. Season well with salt and freshly ground black pepper.

Heat a large frying pan over medium heat and add a tablespoon of oil. Place heaped teaspoons of the mixture into the pan and press down to form flat fritters. As each fritter becomes golden on the bottom, turn and cook until golden on both sides. Remove and drain on paper towels. Repeat this process, adding a little more oil to the frying pan as necessary, and cook the remaining batter. Serve warm accompanied with lemon wedges. Makes 36.

pastry twists

2 teaspoons ground cinnamon
¹/₄ cup caster (superfine) sugar
¹/₂ sheet ready-prepared puff pastry
15 g (¹/₂ oz) butter, melted

Place the cinnamon and sugar in a small bowl and stir to combine. Cut the pastry into 12 x 5 mm (¹/₄ inch) strips, then cut the lengths in half again. Place each of the strips onto a baking tray lined with baking paper, brush with melted butter and sprinkle with some of the cinnamon sugar. Preheat the oven to 160°C (315°F). Gently twist each strip of pastry to form loose spirals, and sprinkle over the top of them any remaining sugar. Refrigerate the pastry twists for 10 minutes. Bake for 10–12 minutes or until lightly golden. Cool on a wire rack. Makes 24. Delicious served with hot chocolate.

pastry twists

all-day
grazing

basics

the casual get-together

Daytime entertaining can be as simple as assembling a wonderful array of flavours and letting everyone help themselves before sitting back and enjoying the afternoon. Pile the table with a few favourite dishes, one or two great cheeses, crusty bread and jugs of chilled drinks.

chill out

Even though 'grazing' by definition denotes a certain casualness in approach, there is no need to forget the finer details that make an occasion feel special. Linen napkins, glistening cutlery and polished glasses are essential, even if it's just a matter of placing a fold-up table in the back yard. Always have chilled water on hand, and whether it's a question of ice buckets or buckets of ice, provide enough of a chill factor to ensure that everyone's drinks are kept icy cool all afternoon.

food to go

If you want to eat alfresco and there isn't a picnic basket in sight, employ other fun ways to transport food. Return to the playground with takeaway boxes filled with a healthy selection of picnic food and labelled with personalised name tags. Line large Chinese steamer baskets with linen napkins and fill with rice paper wraps, hearty rolls, home-baked cake and fresh fruit. Woven storage baskets make for a relaxed take on the traditional. Pile with blankets, glasses, cutlery and bundles of food.

lap lunch

Wrap large soup bowls with napkins and secure each one with a knife and fork, or with chopsticks if serving noodles. When unwrapped, it's an instant table setting in the lap—a great idea not only for picnics but for casual buffet-style lunches. Seek out beautiful fabrics and create visual drama with the colourful stack.

serving solutions

Discard the need for plates and cutlery altogether by providing a selection of favourite salads, some serving spoons, paper napkins and a large bowl of washed lettuce leaves. Allow everyone to help themselves by placing the salads in the centre of the leaves and simply rolling the food up. If kept on ice, this is a very refreshing solution to summer entertaining.

chill out

food to go

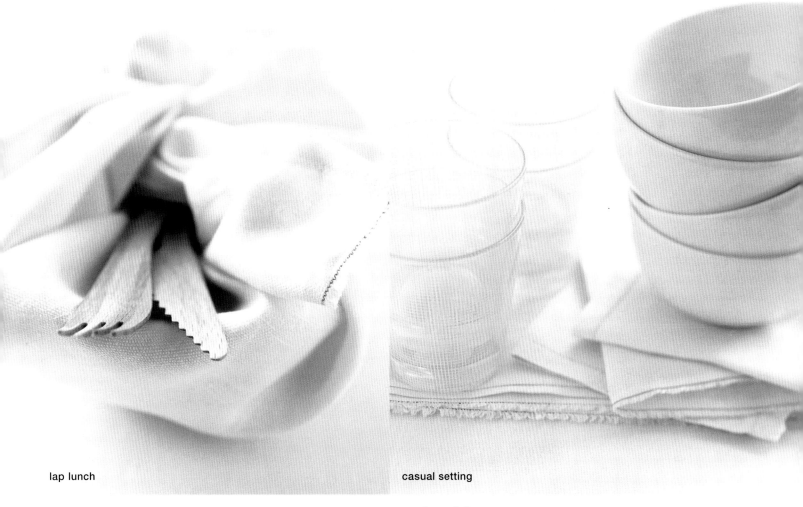

lap lunch

casual setting

serving solutions

good ideas

little bowls

Fill small bowls with everyone's favourite salads, pastas or soups. Try herbed soba noodles, pesto farfalle, orrechiette with fresh tomato sauce, caesar salad, laksa or miso soup.

rice paper wraps

Rice paper parcels are one of the easiest ways to hand around everyone's favourite taste sensations. Soak rice paper rounds in warm water for 1–2 minutes, then fill with duck, mango, snowpea sprouts and a sprinkling of Szechwan peppercorns.

Other fillings you might like to try could include lime-seared prawns with lemon grass and coriander (cilantro), or the classic combination of rice vermicelli, mint, coriander (cilantro) and garlic chives, served with a Thai dipping sauce.

Other great fillings for lavash bread include pastrami with cucumber, dill pickles and roasted capsicum (pepper), and spicy guacamole, coriander (cilantro) leaves and shredded iceberg lettuce.

lavash wraps

Make a meal out of flat breads wrapped around your favourite fillings. Try shredded chicken, lemon mayonnaise*, mango chutney and sprouts, or rare roast beef, spiced beetroot relish and fresh mint.

For other pizza variations, try roasted red capsicum (pepper), artichoke and goat's cheese, or spicy salami, pesto and mozzarella. For a simple but tasty meal, try caramelised brown onion with anchovy, or blue cheese and rocket (arugula).

tiny pizzas

Roll out small circles of pizza dough* and top with a selection of your favourite things. Try prosciutto and fresh figs, or roasted pumpkin, feta, black olives and thyme.

pan bagna

chicken and pine nut salad

green chicken salad

pan bagna

1 thin baguette (French bread stick)
1 tablespoon virgin olive oil
1 clove garlic, peeled and sliced in half
2 red capsicums (peppers), roasted, skin and seeds removed
1 tablespoon salted capers*, rinsed and drained
185 g (6 oz) tin tuna, drained
15 black olives, seeds removed
1/2 small red onion, finely sliced
15 basil leaves
1/2 cup roughly chopped fresh flat-leaf (Italian) parsley
10 anchovies
100 g (3 1/2 oz) marinated artichoke hearts, drained

With a sharp bread knife, slice the baguette in half down its length and remove the bread filling from both the top and bottom portions. Brush the interior of the loaf with olive oil and rub with garlic.
Cut the roasted capsicum into thin strips and combine with the remaining ingredients in a bowl. Season with salt and freshly ground black pepper and spoon inside the bottom half of the loaf, heaping it up. Reassemble the loaf, making sure that the sides meet neatly. Wrap in plastic wrap, place a weight on top (a breadboard or heavy saucepan is suitable) and place in the refrigerator overnight. Slice into 2 cm (3/4 inch) widths and serve. Makes 20 slices.

chicken and pine nut salad

1 egg yolk
1 teaspoon balsamic vinegar
1/2 cup (4 fl oz) light olive oil
2 anchovy fillets, finely chopped
2 chicken breasts (400 g / 13 oz), poached and shredded
1/4 cup salted capers*, rinsed and drained
1/4 cup toasted pine nuts
1/4 cup currants
1/2 cup roughly chopped fresh flat-leaf (Italian) parsley
zest of 1 lemon

Place the egg yolk and vinegar in a small bowl and whisk to combine. Slowly add the oil, whisking continuously to form a thick and creamy mayonnaise. Fold the chopped anchovy fillets through the mayonnaise and season with salt and freshly ground black pepper. Set aside.
Place the remaining ingredients in a large bowl and toss together. Fold in the anchovy mayonnaise. Serve the salad in little bowls and season with cracked black pepper to taste. Makes 15 small or 4 standard serves.

green chicken salad

2 chicken breasts (400 g / 13 oz), poached and shredded
3 spring (green) onions, finely sliced on the diagonal
1/4 cup roughly chopped fresh coriander (cilantro) leaves
1/4 cup roughly chopped fresh mint leaves
1/4 cup dried Asian fried onions*
2 tablespoons toasted sesame seeds
2 tablespoons lime juice
2 tablespoons fish sauce
2 teaspoons grated fresh ginger
2 red chillies, seeded and finely chopped
1 tablespoon palm sugar*

Place the shredded chicken meat, spring onions, coriander, mint leaves, fried onions and sesame seeds in a large bowl and mix together. In a small bowl, mix together the lime juice, fish sauce, ginger, chillies and palm sugar. Stir until the sugar has dissolved and pour over the salad. Makes 15 small or 4 standard serves.

goat's curd, prosciutto and sour cherries on rye

5 slices rye bread, crusts removed
100 g (3 1/2 oz) goat's curd
5 slices prosciutto*, each slice cut into three
1/4 cup finely chopped bottled sour cherries

Cut each slice of bread into three fingers. Spread a little of the goat's curd onto each piece of bread and top with a piece of prosciutto and a teaspoon of chopped sour cherries. Serve immediately with a sprinkle of freshly ground black pepper. Makes 15 pieces.

goat's curd, prosciutto and sour cherries on rye

49

BANANA CARDAMOM LASSI Remove the small seeds from 1 cardamom pod and place them in a blender along with 1 roughly chopped banana, 1/2 cup (4 fl oz) of natural yoghurt and 1 1/2 cups of ice cubes. Blend until smooth. Serve in chilled glasses. Serves 2.

MANGO LASSI In a blender, combine 3/4 cup of roughly chopped mango flesh, 1 teaspoon of honey, 1 teaspoon of lime juice, 1/2 cup (4 fl oz) of natural yoghurt and 1 1/2 cups of ice cubes. Blend until smooth and pour into chilled glasses. Serves 2.

ICED LYCHEE AND MINT Drain 5 lychees from a tin and reserve ¹/₂ cup (4 fl oz) of the syrup. Place the lychees, reserved syrup, 15 large mint leaves, 1 tablespoon of lime juice and 10 ice cubes in a blender and blend until smooth. Pour into chilled glasses. Serves 2.

KIWI AND CITRUS COOLER Segment 1 lime, 1 lemon and 1 orange and freeze in ice-cube moulds filled with water. Blend 2 cups (16 fl oz) of orange juice, 4 peeled kiwi fruit, ¹/₄ cup (2 fl oz) of lime juice and 2 tablespoons of sugar syrup*. Pour into glasses over the citrus cubes. Serves 4.

cumin tortillas with roasted peppers

fried haloumi parcels

cheese, chilli and olive quesadillas

cumin tortillas with roasted peppers

tortillas

2¹/₂ cups plain (all-purpose) flour
¹/₂ teaspoon baking powder
2 teaspoons ground cumin
100 ml (3¹/₂ fl oz) canola oil
1 tablespoon lime juice
²/₃ cup (5¹/₂ fl oz) natural yoghurt

roasted pepper filling

2 roasted capsicums (peppers), skinned
   and seeds removed, sliced into thin strips
10 basil leaves, torn
1 tablespoon balsamic vinegar
350 g (11 oz) tuna fillet, sliced into three lengthways

Sift the flour, baking powder and cumin into a large bowl. Add the oil and mix well to form a dough. In a small bowl, combine the lime juice, yoghurt and ¹/₂ teaspoon of salt. Drizzle over the flour and slowly combine until the dough begins to soften. Gather into a ball and lightly knead until smooth. Divide into 12 portions. Taking one portion at a time, roll out on a floured surface to form a very thin 18 cm (7 inch) circle. Set aside and repeat with the remaining portions, placing baking paper or plastic wrap between each tortilla. Heat a large frying pan over medium heat. Cook the tortillas, turning once, so that each side is golden brown. Remove and keep warm by covering with a tea towel. Toss the capsicum together with the basil, vinegar and 1 teaspoon of salt. Quickly sear the tuna fillets on all sides. Thinly slice and place on the tortillas. Top with some of the roasted pepper filling, roll up and serve. Makes 12.

fried haloumi parcels

5 sheets filo pastry, cut in half to form squares
150 g (5 oz) haloumi cheese*
2 medium-sized ripe tomatoes
80 g (2³/₄ oz) butter, melted
20 flat-leaf (Italian) parsley leaves
10 large mint leaves

Cover the pastry sheets with a damp cloth. Cut the haloumi into ten slices. Cut the tomatoes in half, then slice to form thin wedges. Lightly brush one of the sheets of filo with butter and fold in half to form a rectangle. Lightly butter the top, then place a slice of haloumi in the centre. Top with three wedges of tomato, two parsley leaves, a mint leaf and a sprinkle of ground black pepper. Fold the sides in on the haloumi and then roll up. Repeat the process with the remaining ingredients. Grease a large frying pan and cook the parcels over medium heat until the undersides are golden brown, then flip over to cook the other side. Serve warm, either whole or cut in half. Makes 10 or 20.

cheese, chilli and olive quesadillas

25 g (³/₄ oz) seeded and chopped black olives
1 large red chilli, seeded and chopped
¹/₂ cup (4 fl oz) olive oil
320 g (11 oz) mozzarella cheese*, grated
150 g (5 oz) feta cheese, grated
12 x 20 cm (8 inch) tortillas*
1 bunch fresh coriander (cilantro), leaves picked

Preheat the oven to 180°C (350°F). Place the olives, chilli and oil in a blender and blend to form a flavoured oil. Set aside. Place the grated mozzarella and feta in a bowl and toss to combine.
Place one of the tortillas on a baking tray. Sprinkle with a liberal coating of the mixed cheeses, plus some coriander leaves. Cover with a second tortilla and brush well with the oil mixture. Continue making quesadillas with the remaining ingredients. Place on an oven tray and bake for 7 minutes. Turn the tortillas over and cook for a further 7–8 minutes. Remove from the oven and slice into quarters or eighths. Serve immediately. Makes 24 or 48 pieces.

rose petal sherbet

4 red organic roses, petals removed
1 cup sugar
1 tablespoon rosewater*
2 litres (64 fl oz) sparkling mineral water

Place the rose petals, sugar and 1¹/₄ cups (10 fl oz) of water in a large saucepan and bring to the boil. Reduce the heat and simmer for 8 minutes, or until a light syrup has been made. Remove any scum as it forms. Cool and stir in the rosewater. To serve, pour the syrup into chilled glasses and top with sparkling mineral water. Serves 8.

rose petal sherbet

MOROCCAN MINT TEA Place 4 sprigs of mint, 1 wedge of lemon, 1 star anise, 1/2 cinnamon stick and 1 teaspoon of caster (superfine) sugar in a small glass and top with boiling water. Stir well to dissolve the sugar, and drink while hot. Serves 1.

ORANGE AND ROSEWATER ICE CUBES Follow the rose petal sherbet recipe on page 54 to make rosewater syrup, then add 1 cup (8 fl oz) of water, pour into ice cube trays and freeze. Place the ice cubes into chilled glasses and fill with freshly squeezed orange juice. Serves 6.

ALMOND SHERBET In a saucepan, place 200 ml (6¹/₂ fl oz) of water, 4 tablespoons of almond meal, 1 cup of sugar and 4 split cardamom pods. Boil until the mixture thickens. Cool, add 1 teaspoon of rosewater* and 2 drops of almond essence. Top up with cold sparkling water. Serves 10.

MANDARIN ICE WITH POMEGRANATE Combine 200 ml (6¹/₂ fl oz) of freshly squeezed mandarin juice with 2 tablespoons of sugar syrup* and pour into glasses filled with crushed ice. Squeeze the juice from half a pomegranate, strain and top up each drink. Serves 2.

green papaya salad

pickled swordfish

caesar salad

pickled salmon

green papaya salad

1 small green papaya (approximately 250 g / 8 oz)
1 red chilli, seeded and finely chopped
1/4 cup (2 fl oz) lime juice
2 tablespoons fish sauce
3 tablespoons grated palm sugar*
2 cloves garlic, crushed
2 tablespoons dried Asian fried onions*
1 cup roughly chopped fresh mint leaves
20 butter lettuce leaves, washed and drained

Coarsely grate the green papaya and set to one side.
Make a sauce by combining the chilli, lime juice, fish sauce,
palm sugar and garlic in a small bowl. Stir to dissolve the
palm sugar. Just prior to serving, combine the grated
green papaya, fried onions, mint leaves and the dressing.
Place a tablespoon of the mixture in each of the lettuce
leaves and serve immediately. Makes 20.

caesar salad

10 slices white bread, crusts removed
1 clove garlic, crushed
15 g (1/2 oz) anchovies, shredded
1 egg yolk
1/2 teaspoon Worcestershire sauce
2 tablespoons lemon juice
3/4 cup (6 fl oz) vegetable or light olive oil
1/2 cup grated fresh parmesan cheese
3 mignonette lettuces, leaves washed and drained

Preheat the oven to 150°C (300°F). Slice the bread into
5 mm (1/4 inch) cubes. Place on a baking tray and toast
in the oven until golden. Allow the croutons to cool.
Place the garlic, anchovies, egg yolk, Worcestershire sauce,
lime juice and some freshly ground black pepper in a bowl
and blend together. Whisk the mixture continuously while
slowly pouring in the oil to form a thick mayonnaise. Fold
the parmesan and croutons through the mayonnaise.
Thinly slice any large lettuce leaves and add them to the
mayonnaise. Spoon the mixture into the small lettuce
leaves and serve immediately. Makes approximately 24.

pickled swordfish

50 ml (1 3/4 fl oz) olive oil
2 red onions, thinly sliced
1–2 small red chillies, seeded and finely chopped
2 cloves garlic, minced
300 g (10 oz) ripe tomatoes, finely diced
400 g (13 oz) swordfish fillets, finely diced
1 cup fresh mint leaves
juice of 4 lemons
20 baby mignonette or cos lettuce leaves,
   washed and drained

Heat the olive oil in a frying pan over medium heat, add
the onions and gently cook for 5–7 minutes, stirring
occasionally, until soft and transparent. Stir through the
chillies, garlic, tomatoes and 1 teaspoon of sea salt.
Remove from the heat and set aside to cool.
Place the raw fish pieces in a single layer in a wide
ceramic or glass dish. Cover with the onion mixture and
fresh mint and pour over enough lemon juice to cover
all the ingredients. Cover and leave to marinate in the
refrigerator for 24 hours. To serve, place a small amount
of pickled fish in the centre of each lettuce leaf and season
with a sprinkle of sea salt and some freshly ground black
pepper. Makes 20.

pickled salmon

2 tablespoons sweet Japanese pickled ginger juice*
2 teaspoons pickled ginger*, finely sliced
1 tablespoon grated fresh ginger
1 teaspoon light soy sauce
1 teaspoon fish sauce
2 tablespoons lime juice
100 g (3 1/2 oz) salmon fillet, boned and skin removed
1 tablespoon finely chopped fresh mint leaves
30 witlof (Belgian endive) leaves, washed and drained
2 teaspoons toasted sesame seeds

In a small bowl, combine the ginger juice, pickled ginger,
fresh ginger, soy sauce, fish sauce and lime juice.
Slice the salmon fillet in half lengthways and then slice
each half thinly. Place the salmon in the ginger dressing
and allow to marinate for 5–10 minutes. Add the mint
leaves and toss to combine. Place a tablespoon of the
mixture into each of the witlof leaves. Sprinkle with the
toasted sesame seeds and serve immediately. Makes 30.

prosciutto and mozzarella wraps

lamb cutlets with red and green sauce

bocconcini and tomato in vine leaves

octopus on toast

prosciutto and mozzarella wraps

2 Roma (egg) tomatoes
20 slices prosciutto*, thinly sliced
200 g (6½ oz) mozzarella*

Slice each tomato into ten vertical slices and then cut the slices in half horizontally. Lay a slice of prosciutto on the work surface and place one halved slice of tomato on it, followed by a slice of mozzarella and then another slice of tomato. Season with freshly ground black pepper and roll up firmly to make a little parcel. Repeat with the remaining ingredients. Heat a lightly greased frying pan over medium heat and cook the prosciutto parcels for 2–3 minutes, or until golden brown. Makes 20.

lamb cutlets with red and green sauce

These sauces can be used to accompany grilled lamb cutlets, and each is sufficient to serve with 10–12 cutlets. Serve both sauces at room temperature.

red sauce
500 g (1 lb) Roma (egg) tomatoes, quartered
1 teaspoon sugar
1 tablespoon pomegranate molasses*
10 basil leaves
1 clove garlic
1 teaspoon ground cumin

Preheat the oven to 180°C (350°F). Place the tomato pieces on a baking tray and sprinkle with the sugar and 1 teaspoon of salt. Roast for 40 minutes, or until the tomatoes are beginning to blacken at the edges and dry out. Place the tomatoes in a food processor or blender with the remaining ingredients and blend to form a smooth sauce. Season well with salt and freshly ground black pepper. Makes 1 cup (8 fl oz) of sauce.

green sauce
1 cup fresh flat-leaf (Italian) parsley leaves
30 mint leaves
5 anchovies
1 tablespoon Indian lime pickle*
3 teaspoons lemon juice
½ cup (4 fl oz) olive oil

Place all the ingredients in a food processor or blender and blend until smooth. Makes 1 cup (8 fl oz) of sauce.

bocconcini and tomato in vine leaves

24 packaged vine leaves*
200 g (6½ oz) Roma (egg) tomatoes, finely diced
200 g (6½ oz) bocconcini*, diced
24 large mint leaves
olive oil, for frying
lemon wedges, to serve

Unwrap the vine leaves and soak them for 1 hour in a large bowl filled with boiling water. Remove and gently pat dry. Place a row of tomato dice near one end of each vine leaf. Top with some of the bocconcini, a mint leaf and some freshly ground black pepper. Roll up firmly, folding the edges in as you go. Heat a large frying pan with a little oil and fry each of the parcels for a minute on each side. Serve warm with a squeeze of lemon. Makes 24.

octopus on toast

8 small octopus, cleaned
2 tablespoons red wine vinegar
1 teaspoon dried oregano
1 cup (8 fl oz) olive oil
8 slices thick-sliced white bread, crusts removed
4 cloves garlic
500 g (1 lb) potatoes, boiled and mashed
1 tablespoon lemon juice
¼ cup finely chopped fresh flat-leaf (Italian) parsley
1 tablespoon seeded and finely chopped black olives
2 teaspoons seeded and finely chopped red chilli
1 teaspoon finely chopped lemon zest

Place the octopus in a ceramic or glass bowl. Combine the vinegar, oregano and ¼ cup (2 fl oz) of oil and pour over the octopus. Cover and leave to marinate for 30 minutes. Preheat the oven to 180°C (350°F). Cut each slice of bread into quarters. Place on a baking tray and toast in the oven until golden. Remove and allow to cool on a wire rack. To make the sauce, place the garlic and 1 teaspoon of salt in a mortar and pestle and pound until soft and creamy. Place in a bowl and add the mashed potato and lemon juice. Whisk the mixture continuously while slowly adding the remaining olive oil. When the sauce is light and fluffy, fold in the parsley, olives, chilli and lemon zest. Heat a heavy-based frying pan over high heat and sear the octopus for 2–3 minutes on both sides until coloured. Remove and cut into quarters. Place a heaped tablespoon of the sauce on each of the bread squares and top with the octopus. Makes 32 pieces.

eggplant pinwheels

duck and marmalade turnovers

tiny brioche with garlic shrimp

eggplant pinwheels

2 red capsicums (peppers), trimmed and seeds removed
400 g (13 oz) zucchini (courgettes)
50 large basil leaves
1 tablespoon balsamic vinegar
3 tablespoons olive oil
1 large eggplant (aubergine), thinly sliced lengthways

Grill or roast the capsicums and set aside to cool. With a vegetable peeler, slice the zucchinis into long ribbons, blanch in boiling water for a few seconds and refresh in cold water. Repeat with the basil leaves. Peel the cooked capsicums and slice the flesh in half. Toss with the vinegar. Heat the oil in a large frying pan over medium heat and cook the eggplant slices until soft. Drain on paper towels. Lay a piece of plastic wrap or baking paper on the work surface and arrange a single line of overlapping eggplant slices. Cover with a layer of zucchini, then a layer of capsicum and finally a layer of basil leaves. Roll up firmly to form a thin log. Repeat with the remaining ingredients. Refrigerate until ready to use. Slice and serve. Makes 20.

duck and marmalade turnovers

20 g (3/4 oz) butter
1 cup finely chopped onions
1 clove garlic, crushed
50 g (13/4 oz) pancetta*, finely diced
1 teaspoon fresh thyme leaves
1/2 cup (4 fl oz) red wine
240 g (71/2 oz) duck breast fillet, finely diced
2 tablespoons bitter orange marmalade
1/4 cup almond meal
30 shortcrust* or ready-prepared puff pastry rounds,
    8 cm (3 inches) in diameter
1 egg, beaten

Heat the butter in a small frying pan over medium heat. Add the onion and garlic and cook for 5–7 minutes, or until the onion is transparent. Add the pancetta and thyme and cook for a further 5 minutes before adding the red wine and diced duck breast. Reduce the heat to low and simmer, covered, for 20 minutes, or until the liquid has been absorbed. Remove the cover and return the heat to medium. Add the marmalade and almond meal, stir and cook for 2 minutes, or until the mix has thickened. Remove from the heat and season with salt and black pepper. Set aside to cool. Preheat the oven to 180°C (350°F). Brush the edges of the pastry rounds with beaten egg. Place a heaped teaspoon of the filling in the centre of each pastry round and fold in half. Seal the edges with a fork and place the turnovers on a baking tray lined with baking paper. Brush with more beaten egg and bake for 20 minutes or until golden brown. Makes 30.

tiny brioche with garlic shrimp

1 quantity brioche dough*
1 egg yolk
1 tablespoon milk
90 g (3 oz) butter
3 cloves garlic, crushed
400 g (13 oz) small green (raw) school prawns
    or shrimp, peeled
3 tablespoons lemon juice
1 tablespoon finely chopped fresh flat-leaf
    (Italian) parsley

Remove the brioche dough from the refrigerator and allow to come to room temperature. Oil two mini muffin or patty cake tins. Break off walnut-sized balls of dough and place them into the muffin moulds. Cover with plastic wrap or a cloth and allow them to rise in a warm place for three hours. Preheat the oven to 180°C (350°F). Make an egg wash by whisking the egg yolk with the milk in a small bowl. When the dough has doubled in size, glaze the brioche with the egg wash, then bake for 20–30 minutes or until golden brown. Remove from the oven and allow to cool.
To make the prawn filling, place the butter and garlic in a heavy-based frying pan and cook over moderate heat for 2–3 minutes, or until the garlic has softened and is aromatic. Add the prawns and season with a little sea salt and cracked black pepper. Cook for 3 minutes, turning once, and then add the lemon juice and parsley. Remove the prawns from the pan, reserving the butter sauce. With a sharp knife, remove the tops of the little brioches and remove about a teaspoonful of bread from the centre of each one to make a deep hole. Fill with the warm prawns and spoon over a little of the butter sauce before replacing the lid of each brioche. Makes 36.

seared beef with rocket

350 g (11 oz) beef fillet, trimmed
1 tablespoon olive oil
20 large rocket (arugula) leaves
100 g (31/2 oz) pesto*

Rub 1 tablespoon of freshly ground black pepper into the surface of the beef fillet. Heat the oil in a frying pan over high heat and sear the fillet for 4 minutes on each side, or until nicely coloured. Remove, season with salt, cover with foil and, when cool, slice into 20 very thin slices.
Place the rocket leaves onto a clean surface. On top of each one place a thin slice of beef. Add a teaspoon of pesto and roll up. Serve immediately. Makes 20.

seared beef with rocket

MINT AND ICE CREAM SMOOTHIE In a blender, place 1 cup of vanilla ice cream, 4 ice cubes, 1/4 cup (2 fl oz) of crème de menthe (or other mint-flavoured liqueur) and 6 mint leaves. Blend until smooth, then pour the drink into small, chilled glasses. Serves 2.

SANGRIA In a large jug, place 1 bottle of Rioja or a light red wine, 100 ml (3 1/2 fl oz) of sugar syrup*, 1/4 cup (2 fl oz) of Cointreau, 1/4 cup (2 fl oz) of lemon juice, 1 thinly sliced orange and 1 thinly sliced lime. Stir all the ingredients well and top with ice. Serves 8.

PIMM'S CLASSIC Place ¼ cup (2 fl oz) of Pimm's, 150 ml (5 fl oz) of dry ginger ale and 1 teaspoon of lime juice into a tall, chilled glass and top with ice. Stir to combine, then garnish with thin slices of orange and strips of cucumber. Serves 1.

WATERMELON AND CHILLI COOLER Blend together 2 cups (16 fl oz) of watermelon juice, 2 tablespoons of chilli syrup* and 2 tablespoons of lime juice. Pour into glasses filled with ice, and garnish with sprigs of fresh mint. Serves 2.

spiced pan bread

corn and shrimp pancakes

seared salmon on brioche with saffron mayonnaise

spiced pan bread

1/2 cup (4 fl oz) olive oil

2 cloves garlic, roughly chopped

1 cup sliced spring (green) onions

1 teaspoon ground cumin

1/2 cup fresh flat-leaf (Italian) parsley leaves

1 tablespoon roughly grated fresh ginger

1/2 roasted red capsicum (pepper), skin and seeds removed

1 teaspoon seeded and finely chopped red chilli

2 cups plain (all-purpose) flour

2 teaspoons baking powder

2 tablespoons peanut (groundnut) oil, for frying

Place 1 teaspoon of sea salt, the oil, garlic, spring onions, cumin, parsley, ginger, capsicum and chilli in a food processor and blend to form a smooth paste. Set aside. Sift the flour and baking powder into the bowl of a mixer. With the machine running on a low speed, add 1/3 cup (2 3/4 fl oz) each of hot and cold water in quick succession. As soon as the dough comes together, transfer to a bowl, cover with plastic wrap and allow to rest for 15 minutes. Divide the dough into four pieces. Roll out one piece to form a 20–25 cm (8–10 inch) round. Brush the surface with 2 tablespoons of the spicy paste, roll up into a fat log then form it into a spiral. Tuck the tail end under and lightly flatten the bread. Repeat this process with the remaining pieces of dough. Roll out one of the spirals to form a thin 20 cm (8 inch) circle. Heat a teaspoon of oil in a frying pan and cook over medium heat for 3–4 minutes, or until the bottom is golden. Flip and fry the other side. Remove the bread to a paper towel to drain. Roll and fry the remaining pieces of dough. Serve warm, cut into triangles. Makes 32 triangles.

corn and shrimp pancakes

100 g (3 1/2 oz) green (raw) prawn meat

2 cups corn kernels

2 large eggs

3 tablespoons cornflour (cornstarch)

1/3 cup Asian dried shrimps*

1 cup chopped fresh coriander (cilantro) leaves

2 cloves garlic, minced

2 tablespoons green peppercorns

1 tablespoon sugar

1 tablespoon Worcestershire sauce

1/2 cup (4 fl oz) peanut (groundnut) oil, for frying

Place the prawn meat and half of the corn kernels in a food processor and process to a coarse paste. Remove to a bowl and add the remaining ingredients, mixing well. Heat the oil in a frying pan over moderate heat and cook tablespoons of the mixture in batches, turning the pancakes once until crisp and golden. Serve warm. Makes 40 small pancakes.

seared salmon on brioche with saffron mayonnaise

5 x 2 cm (3/4 inch) slices of brioche loaf, crusts removed

20 strands saffron

2 egg yolks

2 teaspoons lemon juice

200 ml (6 1/2 fl oz) vegetable oil

200 g (6 1/2 oz) salmon fillet

2 teaspoons olive oil, for frying

20 sprigs chervil, to serve

Cut each slice of brioche into four squares. Place the saffron in a small saucepan with 1/4 cup (2 fl oz) of water. Place over medium heat and reduce until only a tablespoon of liquid remains. Remove from the heat and allow to cool. Place the egg yolks and lemon juice in a blender and season with salt and pepper. Blend, and with the motor still running, slowly drizzle in the oil until a thick mayonnaise forms. Pour into a bowl and fold through the saffron water and threads. Set aside. Season the salmon with salt and pepper. Heat the olive oil in a frying pan over high heat and sear the salmon on both sides, turning once. Reduce the heat and cook for a further 5 minutes. Cool and break the fish up into flakes. Lightly toast the brioche squares. Top with a little of the mayonnaise, some salmon and a sprig of chervil. Makes 20.

chilli cornbread

1 cup polenta (cornmeal)

1 cup plain (all-purpose) flour

1 tablespoon baking powder

1 tablespoon sugar

3 eggs, lightly beaten

3/4 cup (6 fl oz) milk

2 tablespoons natural yoghurt

1/4 cup (2 fl oz) olive oil

3/4 cup corn kernels

1/2 red capsicum (pepper), diced

1 small red chilli, seeded and chopped

3 teaspoons finely chopped fresh marjoram

5 spring (green) onions, thinly sliced

1/2 cup grated mozzarella cheese*

Place the polenta, flour, baking powder and sugar in a bowl, make a well in the centre and add the eggs, milk, yoghurt and oil. Mix well. Add the corn, capsicum, chilli, marjoram and spring onions and mix well. Season with salt and pepper. Preheat the oven to 180°C (350°F). Pour the batter into a greased 30 x 20 cm (12 x 8 inch) baking tray and top with the grated mozzarella. Bake for 35 minutes, or until a skewer comes out clean when inserted into the centre. Cool slightly in the tray, then turn out onto a board. Trim the sides and cut into 4 cm (1 1/2 inch) squares. Makes 24.

chilli cornbread

grilled oysters

radishes with butter and brown bread

quail eggs with zaatar mix

oysters with lime

grilled oysters

40 g (1¹/₄ oz) pancetta*, finely diced
¹/₂ cup fresh breadcrumbs
2 tablespoons finely chopped fresh flat-leaf
  (Italian) parsley
20 g (³/₄ oz) unsalted butter, melted
¹/₂ teaspoon Tabasco sauce
1 tablespoon Worcestershire sauce
2 dozen rock oysters
lemon quarters, to serve

Place the pancetta, breadcrumbs and parsley in a small
bowl and mix well. Pour over the melted butter, Tabasco
sauce and Worcestershire sauce and fold through the mix.
Spread a teaspoon of the mixture over each of the oysters
and place under a hot grill for 2 minutes, or until the topping
is golden brown. Remove from the heat and serve with
wedges of fresh lemon. Makes 24.

radishes with butter and brown bread

1 medium-sized ripe tomato
100 g (3¹/₂ oz) butter, softened
2 bunches small radishes
6 slices brown bread, to serve

Remove the seeds from the tomato and finely dice the
flesh. Place in a bowl along with the softened butter and
a teaspoon of sea salt. Stir to combine and place into a
small dish. Serve alongside the radishes with some thinly
sliced brown bread. Serves 6.

quail eggs with zaatar mix

2 tablespoons lightly toasted sesame seeds
1 tablespoon fresh thyme leaves
1 tablespoon powdered sumac*
¹/₂ teaspoon ground roast cumin
24 quail eggs, boiled and shelled

Mix together the sesame seeds and spices along with
1 teaspoon of sea salt and serve in a small bowl
accompanied by the quail eggs.

oysters with lime

1 tablespoon lime juice
1 teaspoon black sesame seeds*
¹/₄ teaspoon sesame oil
1 tablespoon finely diced Lebanese cucumber
2 dozen freshly shucked oysters

Combine the lime juice, sesame seeds, oil and cucumber
in a small bowl. Serve the oysters accompanied with the
dressing. Makes 24.

prawn toasts

250 g (8 oz) green (raw) prawn meat
1 clove garlic, crushed
2 tablespoons chopped shallots (green onions)
1 teaspoon grated fresh ginger
1 teaspoon sugar
1 teaspoon sesame oil
3 teaspoons cornflour (cornstarch)
2 teaspoons finely chopped fresh coriander
  (cilantro) leaves
1 teaspoon grated lemon rind
8 slices white bread, crusts removed
2 tablespoons sesame seeds, to sprinkle
peanut (groundnut) oil, for frying

Place the prawn meat, garlic, shallots, ginger, sugar,
sesame oil, cornflour, coriander, lemon rind and 1 teaspoon
of salt in a food processor and process in short bursts until
the mixture is smooth and well mixed.
Cut each slice of bread into four, spread the prawn mixture
thickly on each square and sprinkle with sesame seeds.
Place oil in a frying pan to a depth of 1 cm (¹/₂ inch). Heat
the oil over moderate heat and cook the bread, prawn side
down, until golden. Turn and quickly cook the other side.
Serve hot. Makes 32.

prawn toasts

spicy nut biscuits

parmesan parchment bread

caper and polenta muffins with smoked salmon

spicy nut biscuits

1 tablespoon grated fresh ginger
1 green chilli, seeded and finely chopped
200 g (6½ oz) raw cashew nuts
100 g (3½ oz) pistachios
200 g (6½ oz) rice flour
1½ teaspoons ground cumin
2 tablespoons roughly chopped fresh coriander
   (cilantro) leaves
1 tablespoon black sesame seeds*
20 g (¾ oz) butter
2 eggs, beaten
150 ml (5 fl oz) vegetable oil

Place the ginger, chilli, cashew nuts, pistachios, rice flour, cumin, coriander, sesame seeds, butter and 2 teaspoons of salt in a food processor. Pulse a few times to grind the nuts, then transfer to a large bowl. Add the eggs and 3 tablespoons of water and stir until the mixture combines and is slightly sticky. Take a heaped teaspoon of the mixture, roll into a ball and flatten slightly. Heat the oil in a deep frying pan or wok over low heat. Take a few of the flattened balls and place them into the oil. Cook for 5 minutes, turning once, until golden brown. Drain on paper towels. Repeat with the remaining mixture. Makes 55.

parmesan parchment bread

20 g (¾ oz) butter
1 cup finely chopped onion
1 teaspoon finely chopped fresh rosemary
½ cup plain (all-purpose) flour
2 tablespoons grated fresh parmesan cheese

Heat the butter in a small frying pan over medium heat, add the onion and rosemary and cook, stirring occasionally, for 10 minutes, or until the onion is slightly caramelised. Remove from the heat, season with 1 teaspoon of salt and some freshly ground black pepper, and set aside to cool. Preheat the oven to 150°C (300°F). In a food processor, pulse the flour and parmesan until the mixture resembles breadcrumbs. Gradually add the onion mix and process until the dough just comes together.
Divide the dough into eighths and roll out each portion very thinly between two sheets of well-floured baking paper. Remove the top sheet from each, place the dough on baking trays and bake in batches for 10 minutes or until golden brown, then turn over and bake for an additional 5 minutes or until crisp. Cool on a wire rack and break into pieces. Serve the parchment bread with caponata* or a favourite dip. Makes 8.

caper and polenta muffins with smoked salmon

1½ cups plain (all-purpose) flour
⅔ cup polenta (cornmeal)
2 teaspoons baking powder
2 tablespoons salted capers*, rinsed and drained
⅓ cup roughly chopped fresh flat-leaf (Italian) parsley
½ teaspoon finely chopped fresh tarragon
1 cup (8 fl oz) milk
2 tablespoons olive oil
1 egg
4 tablespoons sour cream, to serve
180 g (6 oz) smoked salmon, to serve
wasabi roe* or fresh dill, to garnish

Preheat the oven to 180°C (350°F). Place the flour, polenta, baking powder, capers, parsley and tarragon in a bowl and mix well. Season with some freshly ground black pepper. In a jug, whisk together the milk, oil and egg. Pour into the bowl of dry ingredients and fold through until just combined. Spoon the mixture into a greased patty tin and bake for 20 minutes. When completely cool, cut off the tops of the muffins. Top the muffins with sour cream and about 10 g (¼ oz) of smoked salmon per muffin. Garnish with wasabi roe or fresh dill. Makes 18.

sage and polenta madeleines

150 g (5 oz) unsalted butter, softened
2 teaspoons sugar
2 egg yolks
2 eggs
⅓ cup plain (all-purpose) flour
⅓ cup fine polenta (cornmeal)
1¼ teaspoons baking powder
24 small sage leaves

Preheat the oven to 180°C (350°F). Place 30 g (1 oz) of the butter in a small saucepan and cook over high heat until it begins to brown. Remove from the heat and set aside. Cream the remaining butter and the sugar in a mixing bowl until pale and fluffy. Gradually add the yolks and whole eggs, beating well after each addition. Slowly fold in the dry ingredients, plus 1¼ teaspoons each of salt and coarsely ground black pepper.
Grease a madeleine tin with the browned butter, place a sage leaf in the base of each mould and top with a teaspoon of batter. If you don't have a madeleine tin, use a shallow muffin or patty cake tin. Bake for 7–10 minutes, or until the cakes are golden and springy to the touch. Remove from the tray and cool on a wire rack. Makes 24.

sage and polenta madeleines

afternoon tea

basics

afternoon tea

Afternoon tea appears to be fast disappearing from the entertaining vocabulary. However, there's no reason why you shouldn't indulge yourself every once in a while with plates of childhood cupcakes, fine sandwiches and sugary biscuits. Polish the inherited teapot, create an excuse and share the pleasure around.

eastern flavour

Afternoon tea doesn't have to follow the English role model. Invite everyone over for an Eastern-inspired tea party. Minted or spiced teas, green teas, chilled lassis and floral sherbets can be served with spiced biscuits, nut mixes and Asian-style desserts in summer, while in winter, try cardamom-flavoured coffee and syrupy cakes.

infused sugar

If serving a light black tea, herb tea or Middle Eastern-style tea, a nice touch is to infuse the sugar with the predominant flavour of your choice of tea. Place some lemon rind, orange rind, rose petals or a whole fresh vanilla bean into a jar of sugar for a day or two before serving.

tea tools

The basic list of essentials for a tea party is a good teapot, a tea strainer, milk jug, sugar bowl, small plates, tiny napkins, teaspoons and china teacups. It may be mind over matter, but tea always seems to taste nicer out of a fine-lipped teacup. This doesn't necessarily mean an expensive trip to the nearest department store. It's much more interesting to start collecting odd bits and pieces from markets. Find a style that suits you, from funky fifties to all-over floral, and have fun planning your next get-together.

iced treats

Make tiny versions of your favourite cakes and ice them with soft gelato-coloured icing. Decorate them with sugared fresh fruit or crystallised flowers.

quick fix

If you don't have time to make cakes or biscuits, simply cut some puff pastry sheets into 3 x 8 cm (1 1/4 x 3 inch) strips, place onto a greased tray lined with baking paper, and bake in a moderate to hot oven until golden brown. Sprinkle with icing sugar and serve with fresh berries and whipped cream flavoured with natural vanilla extract.

tea tools

infused sugar

iced treats

quick fix

eastern flavour

chicken and herb tea-sandwiches

sago puddings

cucumber tea-sandwiches

spiced treacle tarts

chicken and herb tea-sandwiches

300 g (10 oz) chicken thigh fillet
1/2 cup roughly chopped fresh flat-leaf
  (Italian) parsley
2 teaspoons olive oil
1 teaspoon fresh thyme leaves
2 teaspoons finely chopped fresh chives
2 teaspoons finely chopped fresh mint
50 g (1 3/4 oz) butter, softened
12 thin slices white bread, crusts removed

Preheat the oven to 180°C (350°F). Place the chicken and parsley in a small baking tray, pour over the oil and sprinkle with thyme and 1 teaspoon of salt. Cover with foil and bake for 30 minutes. Allow the chicken to cool, then finely chop or shred the flesh. Fold the chives and mint through the softened butter and spread lightly onto the slices of bread. Divide the chicken equally between six slices of bread, season with salt and freshly ground black pepper and top with the remaining bread slices. Cut each of the sandwiches into four triangles. Serve immediately. Makes 24 triangles.

sago puddings

1/4 cup sago
1/4 cup caster (superfine) sugar
2 cups (16 fl oz) milk
1 sheet leaf gelatine
1/3 cup toasted and crushed hazelnuts
1/4 teaspoon grated nutmeg
2 tablespoons bitter orange marmalade
150 ml (5 fl oz) cream, whipped
fresh berries or poached fruit, to serve

Place the sago, sugar and milk in a saucepan and bring to the boil. Reduce the heat and simmer for 20 minutes, or until the sago is soft and cooked. Remove from the heat and cool slightly. Soak the leaf gelatine in cold water until soft, squeeze off any excess water and add the gelatine to the warm sago mix. Allow to cool completely. When the sago mix has cooled, fold through the hazelnuts, nutmeg and marmalade. Stir to combine all the ingredients, then fold in the whipped cream. Spoon into ten small glasses and chill. To serve, top with fresh berries or poached fruit. Makes 10 small serves.

cucumber tea-sandwiches

2 tablespoons finely chopped fresh dill
50 g (1 3/4 oz) butter, softened, or
  3 tablespoons mayonnaise
12 thin slices of bread, crusts removed
2 Lebanese cucumbers, thinly sliced

Fold the dill through the softened butter or mayonnaise and spread lightly onto the slices of bread. Place the thinly sliced cucumber on six of the bread slices. Season with freshly ground black pepper and top with the remaining bread. Cut each sandwich into three fingers and serve immediately. Makes 18 small slices.

spiced treacle tarts

1/2 cup desiccated coconut
1/2 cup (4 fl oz) golden syrup
1/4 teaspoon ground cardamom
1 tablespoon lime juice
2 teaspoons finely chopped lime zest
1 egg yolk, beaten
24 pre-baked tart shells*
icing (confectioners') sugar, for dusting

Preheat the oven to 180°C (350°F). Place all the ingredients except the tart shells and icing sugar in a bowl and mix well. Spoon a heaped teaspoon of the filling into each of the pastry cases and bake for 10 minutes. Remove and cool on a wire rack. Dust with icing sugar before serving. Makes 24.

lime madeleines

2 eggs
1/4 cup caster (superfine) sugar
1/2 teaspoon finely chopped lime zest
1/2 cup plain (all-purpose) flour
50 g (1 3/4 oz) unsalted butter, melted
1 teaspoon lime juice
1/2 teaspoon orange flower water*
caster (superfine) sugar, extra, to serve

Beat the eggs, caster sugar, lime zest and a pinch of salt in a bowl until the mixture is pale and thick. Sift the flour over the egg mix and lightly fold it in. Gently fold through the butter, lime juice and orange flower water.
Preheat the oven to 200°C (400°F). Grease a madeleine tin and drop a teaspoon of the batter into each of the moulds. If you don't have a madeleine tin, use a shallow muffin or patty cake tin. Bake for 5 minutes. Repeat with any remaining mixture. Turn out onto a wire rack and sprinkle with caster sugar. Makes 36.

lime madeleines

cinnamon jam drops

passionfruit melting moments   shortbread

cinnamon jam drops

3/4 cup self-raising (self-rising) flour
1 teaspoon ground cinnamon
1/4 cup rice flour
75 g (2 1/2 oz) unsalted butter, softened
1/3 cup sugar
1 egg, beaten
berry jam

Preheat the oven to 180°C (350°F). Sift together the flour, cinnamon and rice flour. In another bowl, cream the butter and sugar until light and fluffy, then gradually add the egg, beating well. Fold into the sifted ingredients until just combined. Roll a teaspoon of the batter into a ball and place on a baking tray lined with baking paper. Repeat with the remaining mixture. Press a deep indent into the centre of each ball and fill with a little berry jam. Bake for 8–10 minutes, or until golden. Makes 36.

passionfruit melting moments

125 g (4 oz) unsalted butter, chilled and cubed
1/4 cup icing (confectioners') sugar
3/4 cup plain (all-purpose) flour
1/4 cup cornflour (cornstarch)
1 tablespoon passionfruit pulp
lime butter
60 g (2 oz) unsalted butter, softened
1 cup icing (confectioners') sugar
1 teaspoon grated lime zest
2 teaspoons lime juice
icing (confectioners') sugar, extra,
   for dusting

Preheat the oven to 160°C (315°F). Place the butter, icing sugar, flour and cornflour in a food processor and process in short bursts until the mixture just comes together. Fold through the passionfruit pulp. Pipe the mixture in 1 teaspoon amounts onto a baking tray lined with baking paper. Bake for 15–20 minutes, or until the biscuits are just lightly golden brown. Remove and cool on a wire rack.
To make the lime butter, place the butter, icing sugar and lime zest in a mixing bowl and beat until the mixture is white. Fold through the lime juice.
Stick the biscuits together with lime butter and lightly dust with icing sugar. Makes 36.

shortbread

1 1/2 cups plain (all-purpose) flour
3/4 cup rice flour
200 g (6 1/2 oz) unsalted butter, softened
1/3 cup caster (superfine) sugar
2 teaspoons finely chopped lemon zest
2 tablespoons caster (superfine) sugar, extra, for sprinkling

Preheat the oven to 190°C (375°F). Select a 30 x 20 cm (12 x 8 inch) baking tray and grease and line it with baking paper. Sift the flours, together with a pinch of salt, into a bowl. Cream the butter and sugar until light and fluffy, and fold through the flours until just combined. Press the mixture into a baking tray and prick all over with a fork. Use a sharp knife to mark 3 cm (1 1/4 inch) squares. Bake for 5 minutes, then reduce the oven temperature to 160°C (315°F) and cook for a further 15–20 minutes until the shortbread is a pale golden colour. Sprinkle the lemon zest over the top of the shortbread and cook for a further 5 minutes. Remove from the oven and sprinkle with caster sugar while still warm. Cut into squares and cool on a wire rack. Makes 60.

chocolate creams

1 1/4 cups plain (all-purpose) flour
2 tablespoons Dutch cocoa powder
1 teaspoon baking powder
100 g (3 1/2 oz) unsalted butter
180 g (6 oz) dark chocolate
1/2 cup caster (superfine) sugar
2 eggs
chocolate cream
100 g (3 1/2 oz) chocolate
2 tablespoons cream
cocoa powder, extra, for dusting

Into a bowl, sift together the flour, cocoa, baking powder and 3/4 teaspoon of salt. Melt the butter and chocolate in a medium-sized bowl over a saucepan of simmering water, stirring until smooth. Remove from the heat and add the sugar, stirring until dissolved. Stir in the eggs, one at a time, until well combined, then fold through the dry ingredients. Refrigerate the mixture for 20 minutes or until just firm. Make the chocolate cream by melting the chocolate and cream in a bowl over a saucepan of simmering water, stirring until smooth. Remove from the heat and allow to cool. Preheat the oven to 180°C (350°F). Pipe teaspoon-sized buttons onto baking trays lined with baking paper and bake for 5–7 minutes, or until firm. Cool slightly on the tray before transferring to a wire rack.
Stick the bases of the biscuits together with the chocolate cream and lightly dust with cocoa. Store in an airtight container. Makes 40 biscuits.

chocolate creams

cocktail
hour

basics

chill out

Cocktails are all about icy flavours and cool fun, so invite your friends around and ply them with your latest invention or a classic blend. Whether it's the cocktail hour, a lazy afternoon or a late-night wind-down, this is the time to simply chill out.

shaken or stirred

Martini shakers are not essential but they are useful. The purpose of a shaker is to not only combine the spirits but to chill the alcohol. If no shaker is available, improvise by filling a small jug with lots of ice, adding your cocktail blend and stirring well until the surface of the jug begins to form a frost. Strain the cocktail into a glass and serve immediately.

bar essentials

There are a few must-haves when setting up a bar. Soda water, tonic water, ginger ale, sugar syrup*, fresh lemons and bitters should all be at hand. If you don't have time to make a sugar syrup and you are not embarking upon an evening of frozen daiquiris, caster (superfine) sugar is a suitable substitute.

cocktail accessories

Cocktails are all about the perfect science of matching flavours, so if you are serious about your cocktails, invest in a two-sided measure or jigger. Cocktail spoons, with their long, corkscrew handles, are ideal for stirring drinks and for layering various spirits. Muddlers are wooden pestles, predominantly used for crushing ice, limes and fresh mint. You can easily substitute them with the end of a wooden spoon.

get cool

Ice is essential to any party and comes with its own list of accessories. Always buy more than you think you'll need. Fill ice buckets for easy access during the cocktail hour, and remember to add an ice scoop or ice tongs. If you are doing blended cocktails, always use ice that has been out of the freezer for a few minutes to make for easier blending and smoother drinks.

tools of the trade

Most cocktails involve some form of food preparation, whether it's preparing fruit for blending, making garnishes or slicing and squeezing citrus fruits. Always reserve a small chopping board solely for preparing fruit. A small, sharp knife is essential for any fruit garnishes, while a channel knife will help you to make perfect citrus zest.

tools of the trade

cocktail accessories

shaken or stirred

get cool

bar essentials

party basics

how to party

When planning a serious cocktail party, it is essential to choose the cocktails which will be served during the evening.
With a small selection of drinks you can do a lot of the organising in advance. Pre-cut all the fruit and squeeze the
lemon or lime juice in advance. Organise the glasses so that they are within easy reach, and check that you have
enough glasses to cover the selection, remembering that most guests will probably try all the cocktails on offer.
Always have plenty of cocktail napkins available, and enough food to soak up the heady concoctions.

flea-market finds

With a little bit of advance notice, it's fun to shop for
your party in the local markets and junk stores. Make
a beeline for funky glasses, sixties bar accessories,
interesting swizzle sticks and classic martini shakers.
With any luck you'll find an old Dean Martin LP and
some Rat Pack attitude.

light sources

How you light a room, garden
or house is intrinsic to creating
atmosphere. There are so
many options: strings of fairy
lights, Chinese lanterns, tea-
lights, home-made lanterns,
large candles, floating candles,
clusters of candles, Mexican
lanterns and lava lamps. The
only hard-and-fast rule is to
keep the electric lights low
and the candles burning.

mocktails

Nowadays, with changing drinking
patterns and an awareness of health
issues, it is important to always have a
non-alcoholic option. With such great
fruits available, it's not difficult to invent
a mocktail of the moment.

music

Music is one of the most important elements to any party. It sets the tone and carries
the changing ambience of the evening, and if it's good, the party can't possibly fail.
Remember that the music you listen to every day isn't necessarily great party music, so
do some research and invest in a few good mixes that suit the mood you want to create.

flea-market finds

how to party

light sources

mocktails

music

good ideas

glass rims

Rub lime or lemon along the rim of a cocktail glass and upend into a saucer filled with spiced salt or sugar. Shake the glass free of any excess seasoning and prepare to make your cocktail.

flavoured ices

Fill ice-cube trays with fresh fruit juice to add to your favourite drink, or suspend a favourite garnish in ice. Serve in individual drinks, or fill a jug and top with a cocktail blend or fresh juice.

fruit garnishes

For some people it just isn't a real cocktail unless there's half a fruit bowl spiralling off the rim. However, if you want to make a statement, simply break with tradition and garnish your martini with a caperberry or a twist of tangelo.

drunken fruits

Marinate cherries, berries, tiny peeled pears or stone fruit for several hours in your liqueur of choice and serve as a cocktail garnish.

flavoured syrups

Any spirit or syrup can be flavoured with a variety of fruits and spices, from chilli through to cherry. Place your chosen flavouring into your favourite spirit and allow to infuse for a month.

garnishes

Garnishes can be as simple as the perfectly placed olive or as garish as your sense of kitsch allows. Start collecting swizzle sticks, paper parasols and wacky coasters.

citrus stirrers

Garnish citrus-based drinks with long spirals of sugared zest. Make candied zest* and wrap the long spirals around chopsticks before dredging in caster (superfine) sugar. Allow to dry overnight on a bed of sugar.

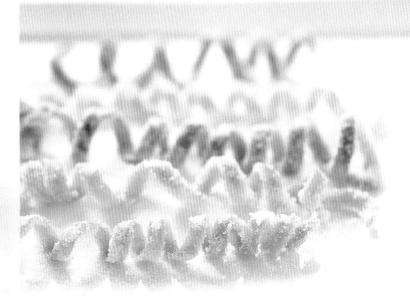

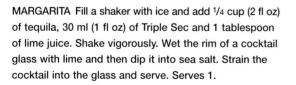

MARGARITA Fill a shaker with ice and add ¼ cup (2 fl oz) of tequila, 30 ml (1 fl oz) of Triple Sec and 1 tablespoon of lime juice. Shake vigorously. Wet the rim of a cocktail glass with lime and then dip it into sea salt. Strain the cocktail into the glass and serve. Serves 1.

FRUIT DAIQUIRI In a blender, place 30 ml (1 fl oz) of lime juice, 2 teaspoons of sugar, 2 teaspoons of Triple Sec or Cointreau, ½ cup (4 fl oz) of white rum, ½ cup each of diced mango and honeydew, and 6 ice cubes. Blend and pour into two chilled glasses. Serves 2.

CLASSIC DAIQUIRI Fill a cocktail shaker with ice and add 1/4 cup (2 fl oz) of rum, 1 tablespoon of lime juice, 1 teaspoon of Triple Sec and 1 teaspoon of caster (superfine) sugar. Shake well and strain into a chilled cocktail glass. Serves 1.

COSMOPOLITAN Fill a cocktail shaker with ice and add 1/4 cup (2 fl oz) of vodka, 30 ml (1 fl oz) of Cointreau, 1 teaspoon of lime juice and 30 ml (1 fl oz) of cranberry juice. Shake vigorously, then strain into a chilled cocktail glass. Serves 1.

spiced nut blend

1 teaspoon cumin seeds
1 teaspoon coriander seeds
1 teaspoon mustard seeds
1/4 teaspoon fennel seeds
1/2 cinnamon stick
1/2 teaspoon black peppercorns
1 teaspoon ground turmeric
2 tablespoons brown sugar
350 g (11 oz) mixed nuts, including pecans, cashews,
   peanuts (groundnuts) and macadamias
2 tablespoons olive oil

Preheat the oven to 160°C (315°F). Place all the spices in a spice grinder or blender and grind to a fine powder. Transfer the mixture to a large bowl and mix through the brown sugar, nuts and 2 teapoons of sea salt. Add the olive oil, mix well and place on a baking tray. Bake for 10–15 minutes, or until the nuts have coloured a little, stirring occasionally. Allow to cool. Store in an airtight container until ready to serve. Makes 350 g (11 oz).

spiced potato crisps

1 teaspoon sesame seeds
1/2 teaspoon ground cumin
1/2 teaspoon ground coriander
1/2 teaspoon paprika
2 large potatoes, peeled
20 g (3/4 oz) unsalted butter, melted

Preheat the oven to 170°C (325°F). Combine the spices and herbs in a small bowl. Slice the potatoes very thinly and place half the slices on a baking tray lined with baking paper. Top each slice of potato with another slice, preferably of a similar size, and press together. (The starch in the potatoes will stick them together.) Brush with butter and sprinkle with the spice mix.
Bake for 45 minutes, or until the potatoes are crisp and golden brown. Drain on paper towels and serve.
Makes approximately 30 crisps.

fried green olives

1/4 cup finely chopped fresh flat-leaf (Italian) parsley
1/3 cup feta cheese, crumbled
20 large green olives, stones removed
1/4 cup plain (all-purpose) flour
1 egg, beaten
1/2 cup fine breadcrumbs
100 ml (31/2 fl oz) vegetable oil

Place the parsley and feta in a bowl and stir well, then stuff a little of the mixture into the centre of each of the olives. Place the flour in a shallow bowl, the egg in a small bowl and the breadcrumbs in another bowl. Heat the oil in a deep frying pan over medium heat. Toss the olives, a few at a time, in the flour, then dip into the beaten egg and finally roll in the breadcrumbs. Fry in the oil for 1 minute, or until golden brown. Remove from the pan and drain on paper towels. Repeat with the remaining olives. Makes 20.

parmesan biscuits

125 g (4 oz) butter, chilled and cubed
1/2 cup grated cheddar cheese
1/2 cup grated fresh parmesan cheese
150 g plain (all-purpose) flour
1 teaspoon paprika

Place all the ingredients and 1/4 teaspoon of salt in a food processor. Using the pulse action, process until the ingredients just combine. Remove the dough and form it into a ball. Divide in half, then roll and shape each portion into a sausage about 23 cm long x 3 cm wide (9 x 11/4 inches). Roll in baking paper and chill for 1 hour. The dough can be frozen at this point until ready to use.
Preheat the oven to 180°C (350°F). Remove the baking paper from the dough rolls and cut each portion into 5 mm (1/4 inch) slices. Place on a baking tray lined with baking paper and bake for 12–15 minutes, or until pale gold in colour. Cool on a wire rack. Repeat until all the biscuits are cooked. Store in an airtight container until ready to serve. Makes 65–70.

spiced nut blend

fried green olives

spiced potato crisps

parmesan biscuits

martini

champagne cocktail

bellini

martini

1 teaspoon dry vermouth
ice, to fill cocktail shaker
1/4 cup (2 fl oz) gin
an olive or lemon peel, for garnish

Place a teaspoon of vermouth into a chilled martini glass. Fill a cocktail shaker with ice and add the gin. Swirl the vermouth around the glass, then pour it out. Strain the iced gin into the glass and serve immediately with a garnish of an olive or lemon peel. Serves 1.

champagne cocktail

1 sugar cube
3 dashes Angostura bitters
3 teaspoons brandy
champagne

Moisten the sugar cube with the bitters and place in a champagne flute. Pour in the brandy and top with champagne. Serves 1.

bellini

1/2 ripe white peach
1 teaspoon caster (superfine) sugar
champagne

Purée the peach and sugar and set aside. Pour a little champagne into two champagne flutes and divide the peach purée between the glasses. Lightly stir, then top with the champagne. Serves 2.

manhattan

1/4 cup (2 fl oz) blended whisky
30 ml (1 fl oz) sweet vermouth
dash of Angostura bitters
lemon peel, for garnish

Fill a glass with ice, then add the whisky, vermouth and bitters. Stir until the alcohol has chilled, then strain into a chilled cocktail glass. Serve with a twist of lemon peel. Serves 1.

manhattan

whiting and pumpkin tempura

300 g (10 oz) Japanese pumpkin, peeled
10 large whiting fillets, bones removed
2 tablespoons lemon juice
1/3 cup (2 3/4 fl oz) soy sauce
2 tablespoons mirin*
2 teaspoons pickled ginger juice*
1 1/4 cups tempura flour*
500 ml (16 fl oz) canola oil, for deep-frying
fresh coriander (cilantro) leaves, to garnish

Slice the pumpkin into 20 x 2–3 mm (1/8 inch) slices and set aside. Slice the whiting fillets in half lengthways. Make the dipping sauce by combining the lemon juice, soy sauce, mirin and pickled ginger juice in a small bowl. Set aside. Place the tempura flour in a bowl, add 1 cup (8 fl oz) of iced water and stir gently with chopsticks until the mixture is just combined and slightly lumpy.
Heat the oil in a wok or deep frying pan over medium heat. Dip the pumpkin slices in the batter and cook in batches for 2–3 minutes, or until lightly golden. Dip the whiting in the batter and cook in batches until lightly golden. Dip the coriander leaves in the batter and cook for a few seconds. Drain all tempura and serve immediately, accompanied with the dipping sauce. Makes 40 pieces.

baby eggplant with grilled miso

80 g (2 3/4 oz) white miso*
1 tablespoon sugar
1 tablespoon mirin*
1 egg yolk
2 teaspoons fresh ginger juice*
10 baby eggplants (aubergines)
200 ml (6 1/2 fl oz) vegetable oil
1 tablespoon sesame seeds

Place the miso, sugar and mirin in a large bowl, add the egg yolk and lightly whisk. Place the bowl over a saucepan of boiling water, whisking continuously while you slowly add 1/3 cup (2 3/4 fl oz) of cold water. Keep whisking until the mixture is thick and creamy. Stir through the ginger juice. Preheat the oven to 190°C (375°F). Slice each of the eggplants in half lengthways and trim the skin side so that the halves will sit flat. Heat the oil in a deep frying pan over moderate heat and cook the eggplants on both sides until they are golden and slightly soft. Remove and drain on paper towels. Place the eggplants on a baking tray and spread with a little of the miso paste you have made. Sprinkle with sesame seeds and bake for 5 minutes. Makes 20.

sashimi tuna with spinach and sesame

200 g (6 1/2 oz) sashimi tuna
1 bunch fresh English spinach, washed well
1 teaspoon caster (superfine) sugar
2 tablespoons soy sauce
4 tablespoons sesame seeds
2 teaspoons mirin*

Place the tuna in the freezer for 30–35 minutes. (This firms the tuna flesh, making it easier to slice thinly.) Plunge the spinach leaves into salted boiling water for 20 seconds, then remove and place in a bowl of iced water. Drain and squeeze out any excess water before shredding finely. In a small bowl, dissolve the sugar in the soy sauce. Toast the sesame seeds in a frying pan over medium heat, removing from the heat when they begin to pop. Roughly grind or chop the seeds and place them in a small bowl along with the mirin, soy sauce and sugar mixture, and the spinach. With a sharp knife, slice the tuna very thinly to make approximately 30 slices. Place one of the slices onto a clean work surface. Take a teaspoon of the spinach, squeeze it of any liquid and place it at one end of the tuna. Roll up and place on a serving platter. Repeat with the remaining tuna and spinach. Serve immediately. Makes 30.

prawn balls

1/4 cup rice flour
24 large green (raw) prawns, shelled and deveined
2 1/2 teaspoons mirin*
1 egg white, lightly beaten
1/3 cup finely sliced spring (green) onions
100 g (3 1/2 oz) somen noodles*, broken into small pieces
2 tablespoons lime juice
2 tablespoons mirin*, extra, for sauce
4 tablespoons soy sauce
100 ml (3 1/2 fl oz) peanut (groundnut) oil

Sift the flour and 1/4 teaspoon of salt into a bowl. Make a well in the centre and gradually add 2 tablespoons of water, whisking to make a smooth paste. Set aside.
Mince or finely chop the prawn meat, place in a bowl and stir through the mirin, egg white, spring onions and the flour paste. Season with salt and freshly ground black pepper and mix well to combine.
Spread the broken noodles on a sheet of baking paper. Roll 1/2-tablespoon amounts of the prawn mix into balls and then roll them in the broken noodles. Set aside.
Make a sauce by combining the lime juice, mirin and soy. Heat the oil in a wok or deep frying pan over medium heat and cook the prawn balls until they are golden, turning if necessary. Drain on paper towels and serve with the dipping sauce. Makes 12.

whiting and pumpkin tempura

sashimi tuna with spinach and sesame

baby eggplant with grilled miso

prawn balls

pistachio and orange crackers

gravlax with dill dressing on pumpernickel

bread sticks

pistachio and orange crackers

1 cup plain (all-purpose) flour
1/4 cup rice flour
1/4 teaspoon baking powder
2 teaspoons chopped orange zest
1/4 cup chopped pistachios
3 tablespoons vegetable oil
100 ml (3 1/2 fl oz) natural yoghurt
1 egg white, lightly whisked

Preheat the oven to 180°C (350°F). Sift the flours, baking powder and 1 1/2 teaspoons of salt into a bowl. Add the orange zest, pistachios and some freshly ground black pepper and mix well. Add the oil and yoghurt and mix to form a dough. Lightly knead until smooth, then place on a floured surface and roll out as thinly as possible. Cut out crackers with a 4 cm (1 1/2 inch) round cookie cutter or into 4 cm (1 1/2 inch) squares and brush with the egg white. Place onto baking trays lined with baking paper and cook in batches in the oven for 15 minutes or until golden brown. Cool on wire racks. Delicious with a sharp cheddar or with crème fraîche* and smoked trout. Makes 30.

gravlax with dill dressing on pumpernickel

1 egg yolk
1 teaspoon grain mustard
1 tablespoon lemon juice
1/2 teaspoon sugar
1/4 cup (2 fl oz) olive oil
3/4 cup (6 fl oz) vegetable oil
3 teaspoons finely chopped fresh dill
150 g (5 oz) gravlax* or smoked salmon
30 small slices pumpernickel*

Whisk together the egg yolk, mustard, lemon juice, sugar and 1/2 teaspoon of salt in a bowl. Mix the oils together in a jug and slowly pour into the egg yolk mixture, whisking continuously until all the oil is incorporated and the dressing thickens. Fold through the finely chopped dill and set aside. Divide the gravlax or salmon between the sliced bread and spoon a little of the dressing over. Season with freshly ground black pepper and serve. Makes 30 pieces.

bread sticks

7 g (1/4 oz) active dry yeast (1 sachet)
1/2 teaspoon sugar
2 1/2 cups plain (all-purpose) flour
2 tablespoons black sesame seeds*
1 tablespoon freshly ground cumin seeds
2 tablespoons chopped fresh thyme
1 egg
1 tablespoon olive oil

In a small bowl, mix the yeast, 1 cup (8 fl oz) of warm water and the sugar. Leave to sit for 5–10 minutes or until the surface begins to froth. Place the flour, sesame seeds, cumin, thyme and 1/2 teaspoon of salt in a large bowl and make a well in the centre. Pour in the yeast mixture and mix to form a soft dough. Gather into a ball, turn out onto a lightly floured surface and knead for 8–10 minutes, or until the dough is smooth and elastic. Place in an oiled bowl and cover with plastic wrap. Leave for 3 hours in a warm place. When doubled in size, punch down and turn out onto a floured surface, then knead lightly for 1–2 minutes. Roll the dough out to a thickness of 5 mm (1/4 inch) and cut into strips approximately 25 cm long x 1 cm wide (10 x 1/2 inch). Roll lightly and place onto baking trays lined with baking paper. Cover and allow to rise for a further 30 minutes. Preheat the oven to 180°C (350°F). In a small bowl, beat the egg with 1/4 cup (2 fl oz) of water. Brush the dough with the egg wash. Place in the oven and bake for 15 minutes or until golden. Remove from the oven, brush the bread sticks with olive oil and sprinkle with sea salt. Return to the oven for a further 4–5 minutes until golden brown. Remove from the oven and allow to cool on a wire rack. Store in an airtight container until ready to use. Makes 30–35.

goat's cheese tartlets

150 g (5 oz) goat's cheese
1 cup (8 fl oz) cream
1 egg, beaten
3 egg yolks
36 small filo pastry tart shells*

Preheat the oven to 180°C (350°F). Crumble the goat's cheese into a bowl. Slowly add the cream, mashing with a fork until the mixture is smooth and creamy. Fold in the egg and egg yolks and season well with salt and freshly ground black pepper. Pour the mix into the tart shells and bake for 12 minutes or until puffed up and golden. Makes 36.

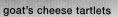
goat's cheese tartlets

mai tai

watermelon, mint and vodka

campari classic

mojito

mai tai

ice, to fill cocktail shaker
1 tablespoon lime juice
2 tablespoons Grand Marnier
dash of Angostura bitters
1/4 cup (2 fl oz) dark Jamaican rum
1 teaspoon grenadine syrup
1/3 cup (2 3/4 fl oz) fresh pineapple juice
2 drops almond essence
ice, extra, to serve
pineapple and mint, to garnish

Fill a cocktail shaker with ice. Add all the remaining ingredients except the extra ice and the garnishes, and shake well. Pour over ice and garnish with fresh pineapple and mint. Serves 1.

campari classic

1/2 cup (4 fl oz) freshly squeezed orange juice
1/4 cup (2 fl oz) Campari
6 ice cubes
sliced orange, to garnish

Pour the orange juice and Campari into a tall glass and top with ice. Garnish with sliced orange. Serves 1.

watermelon, mint and vodka

2 sprigs mint
5 watermelon juice ice cubes
1/2 cup (4 fl oz) watermelon juice
1/2 teaspoon lime juice
30 ml (1 fl oz) vodka

Place the mint sprigs and the watermelon ice cubes in a tall glass and pour over the watermelon juice, lime juice and vodka. Stir well. Serves 1.

mojito

4 sprigs mint
2 teaspoons sugar
1/2 lime, quartered
1/4 cup (2 fl oz) white rum
4 ice cubes
soda water

Place the mint, sugar and lime in a glass and crush well with a muddler or the back of a wooden spoon. Add the rum and ice, and top with soda water. Serves 1.

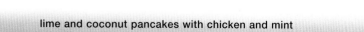

lime and coconut pancakes with chicken and mint

ma hor on pineapple   seared tuna with lime leaf and peanuts

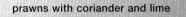

prawns with coriander and lime

lime and coconut pancakes with chicken and mint

2/3 cup (5 1/2 fl oz) lime juice
2 teaspoons sesame oil
2 tablespoons palm sugar*
2 teaspoons fish sauce
1 teaspoon red chilli, seeded and finely chopped
400 g (13 oz) chicken, poached and shredded
1 cup plain (all-purpose) flour
1 egg, lightly beaten
1 lime, zested and juiced
1 cup (8 fl oz) coconut milk
2/3 cup fresh mint leaves
2/3 cup fresh coriander (cilantro) leaves

Combine the lime juice, sesame oil, sugar, fish sauce and chilli in a bowl and stir to dissolve the sugar. Add the chicken. Make the pancakes by sifting the flour and 1/4 teaspoon of salt into a bowl. Make a well in the centre and stir in the egg, zest, juice and coconut milk. Whisk to form a smooth batter. Grease a large non-stick frying pan and heat over low heat. Drizzle in the batter in a cobweb of lines, making a circle 10 cm (4 inches) in diameter. Leave to cook for 2 minutes, then flip and cook for a further 1–2 minutes or until golden. Transfer to a plate and repeat with the remaining pancake mixture. Prior to serving, toss the mint and coriander leaves through the chicken. Fill each of the pancakes with some of the chicken salad, roll up and serve immediately. Makes 20.

ma hor on pineapple

2 cloves garlic, roughly chopped
2 tablespoons roughly chopped fresh coriander (cilantro) root
1/2 teaspoon green peppercorns
1 teaspoon grated fresh ginger
2 spring (green) onions, chopped
2 tablespoons peanut (groundnut) oil
150 g (5 oz) pork mince (ground pork)
75 g (2 1/2 oz) minced prawn meat
1/2 teaspoon finely chopped kaffir lime leaves
1 1/2 tablespoons palm sugar*
1 1/2 tablespoons fish sauce
1 pineapple, quartered, core removed
2 chillies, seeded and finely sliced, to garnish

Place the garlic, coriander root, peppercorns, ginger, spring onions and oil in a blender and pulse until smooth. Heat a frying pan over medium heat, add the paste and cook for 2 minutes. Add the pork and prawn meat and continue to cook, stirring occasionally, until the meat has coloured. Add the lime leaves, sugar and fish sauce, reduce the heat and cook until the mixture is slightly sticky. Allow to cool. Slice the quartered pineapple into 1 cm (1/2 inch) thick triangles, top with the cooled mixture and garnish with chilli. Makes 20.

seared tuna with lime leaf and peanuts

50 ml (1 3/4 fl oz) tamarind water*
1 tablespoon palm sugar*, roughly chopped
1/3 cup (2 3/4 fl oz) lime juice
1 tablespoon grated fresh ginger
1 tablespoon fish sauce
2 teaspoons sesame oil
1 red chilli, seeded and finely chopped
1 tablespoon finely chopped kaffir lime leaves
1 tablespoon finely chopped lemon grass, white part only
300 g (10 oz) tuna fillet, sliced lengthways into three pieces
3 thin Lebanese cucumbers
1/2 cup fresh coriander (cilantro) leaves
1/2 cup peanuts (groundnuts), toasted and finely chopped

Place the tamarind water, palm sugar, lime juice, ginger, fish sauce, sesame oil, chilli, lime leaves and lemon grass in a small bowl and stir well to dissolve the palm sugar. Lightly grease a frying pan, place over high heat and sear the tuna fillets for 1 minute on each side. Remove from the heat and season with a little sea salt. Slice the cucumbers into 1/2–1 cm (1/4–1/2 inch) rounds and top with a slice of tuna. Toss the coriander leaves and peanuts through the dressing and place a teaspoon of dressing onto each of the tuna slices. Serve immediately. Makes 30.

prawns with coriander and lime

2 tablespoons chopped fresh coriander (cilantro) root
2 tablespoons grated fresh ginger
2 cloves garlic, roughly chopped
1 lemon grass stalk, white part only, roughly chopped
1/2 cup (4 fl oz) vegetable oil
1 teaspoon ground coriander
20 large green (raw) prawns, shelled and deveined
1 cup fresh coriander (cilantro) leaves
1/4 cup (2 fl oz) lime juice
1/2 cup (4 fl oz) olive oil
1/2 teaspoon sugar
20 small bamboo skewers, soaked in hot water
 for 20 minutes

Place the coriander root, ginger, garlic, lemon grass, oil and ground coriander in a blender and blend to form a smooth paste. Place the prawns in a ceramic or glass dish and pour over the paste. Allow them to marinate, covered in the refrigerator, for at least an hour.
Blend the coriander leaves, lime juice, olive oil, sugar and a pinch of salt together and set aside. Place a prawn on each of the bamboo skewers and grill on a moderately hot preheated barbecue for 5 minutes. Serve with a drizzle of the coriander dressing. Makes 20.

steamed salmon with fennel and mint

steamed prawn wontons with a lemon dipping sauce   scallop and coriander wontons

steamed salmon with fennel and mint

2 teaspoons mustard seeds
1/2 teaspoon fennel seeds
2 teaspoons sugar
2 tablespoons olive oil
1/2 teaspoon white vinegar
1 cup coarsely grated fennel
1 cup finely sliced Lebanese cucumber
1/3 cup finely sliced fresh mint
1/3 cup (2 3/4 fl oz) lemon juice
200 g (6 1/2 oz) salmon fillet, skin and bones removed
20 scallop shells or Chinese spoons

Place the mustard and fennel seeds, the sugar and 1/4 teaspoon of salt in a mortar and pestle and grind until the fennel seeds have been crushed. Add the oil and vinegar and stir to form a thick dressing. Combine the fennel, cucumber, mint and lemon juice in a bowl. Pour the dressing over the salad and mix well. Slice the salmon into ten thin strips and then slice each in half again, giving you twenty 4 cm x 8 cm x 5 mm (1 1/2 x 3 x 1/4 inch) pieces. Place a piece of salmon on each of the shells or spoons and place in a bamboo steamer over a large saucepan of boiling water. Cover and steam for 2 minutes. Remove from the basket and top with the fennel salad. Serve immediately. Makes 20.

steamed prawn wontons with a lemon dipping sauce

450 g (14 oz) green (raw) prawns, shelled and minced, or 210 g (7 oz) minced prawn meat
1/4 teaspoon five-spice powder
1/2 cup spring (green) onions, finely sliced
2 egg whites
1 teaspoon grated fresh ginger
1 egg
30 square wonton wrappers*
lemon dipping sauce*

Place the prawn meat, five-spice powder, spring onions, egg whites, ginger and 1/2 teaspoon of sea salt in a bowl and stir to combine. Lightly beat the egg with 1/4 cup (2 fl oz) of water in a small bowl.
Place one of the wonton wrappers onto a clean surface and place 1 heaped teaspoon of prawn mixture into the centre. Brush some of the egg wash along the edges and bring the four corners together, sealing the sides. Brush with a little more egg wash and wrap the edges around the dumpling, forming a neat parcel. Repeat with the remaining mixture. Place the dumplings in a bamboo steamer over a large saucepan of boiling water. Cover and steam for 3 minutes. Remove and serve with lemon dipping sauce. Makes 30.

scallop and coriander wontons

400 g (13 oz) white scallop meat, finely diced
1/2 teaspoon grated orange rind
3 tablespoons finely chopped fresh coriander (cilantro) leaves
1/4 cup finely sliced spring (green) onions
1/4 teaspoon sesame oil
2 teaspoons finely chopped red chillies
1 teaspoon fish sauce
1 kaffir lime leaf, shredded
1/4 teaspoon grated fresh ginger
2 tablespoons plain (all-purpose flour)
1 egg
30 square wonton wrappers*
peanut (groundnut) oil, for deep-frying
limes, quartered, to serve

Combine the scallop meat, rind, coriander, spring onions, sesame oil, chilli, fish sauce, lime leaf and ginger in a bowl. Sprinkle the flour over the top, season and stir well. Lightly beat the egg with 1/4 cup (2 fl oz) of water. Place a wonton wrapper on a clean surface and place 1 heaped teaspoon of the scallop mixture into the centre. Brush the egg wash along the edges and bring the corners together, sealing the sides, then twist the top firmly. Repeat with the remaining mixture. Heat the oil in a wok and cook the wontons until golden brown. Remove and serve with lime. Makes 30.

coconut and ginger pancakes with five-spice duck

1 Chinese barbecued duck, skin and flesh shredded
2 teaspoons Chinese five-spice powder
1 cup rice flour
1 3/4 cups (14 fl oz) coconut milk
1 egg, beaten
1 tablespoon grated palm sugar*
1 teaspoon grated fresh ginger
1–2 tablespoons peanut (groundnut) oil
1 cup fresh coriander (cilantro) leaves
hoisin or plum sauce, to serve

Place the duck skin on a baking tray and grill for 1–2 minutes, or until crisp. Place in a bowl. Add the shredded duck meat and any meat juices. Stir in the five-spice powder. Make the pancakes by sifting the rice flour and 1/4 teaspoon of salt into a bowl. Make a well in the centre and stir in the coconut milk, egg, sugar and ginger. Whisk to form a smooth batter. Heat the oil in a frying pan over moderate–high heat. Place 2–3 coriander leaves in the centre and drizzle 2 tablespoons of the batter over them to form a pancake 10 cm (4 inches) in diameter. Cook until the edges start to go crisp. Turn and cook the other side. Repeat with the remaining batter. Place some of the duck mix along one end of each pancake and top with hoisin or plum sauce. Roll up and serve. Makes 20.

coconut and ginger pancakes with five-spice duck

pina colada

1/2 cup fresh pineapple pieces
1 cup ice cubes
2 tablespoons lime juice
1/4 cup (2 fl oz) sugar syrup*
1/4 cup (2 fl oz) white rum
1/4 cup (2 fl oz) coconut cream
fresh pineapple and lime, to garnish

Place all the ingredients except the garnishes in a blender and blend until smooth. Pour into cocktail glasses and decorate with pineapple wedges and thinly sliced lime. Serves 2.

pimm's with ginger syrup

1/2 cup (4 fl oz) fresh pineapple juice
1 1/2 tablespoons ginger syrup*
1/4 cup (2 fl oz) Pimm's
4–5 ice cubes
1/4 cup (2 fl oz) soda water
lime and fresh pineapple, to garnish

Place the pineapple juice, ginger syrup and Pimm's into a tall glass with ice. Top with soda water and garnish with lime and pineapple. Serves 1.

tropical rum blend

30 ml (1 fl oz) white rum
30 ml (1 fl oz) Malibu
30 ml (1 fl oz) Midori
200 ml (6 1/2 fl oz) grapefruit juice
1 cup peeled and roughly chopped honeydew melon
ice, to serve
honeydew melon wedges, to garnish

Place all the ingredients except the ice and honeydew wedges in a blender and blend until smooth. Pour into two tall glasses over ice and garnish with wedges of honeydew. Serves 2.

lychee and rum blast

10 tinned lychees, seeded and chilled
1/3 cup (2 3/4 fl oz) coconut milk, chilled
1/4 cup (2 fl oz) dark rum
1/4 cup (2 fl oz) lychee syrup, chilled
10 mint leaves

Place all the ingredients in a blender and blend until smooth. Pour into two chilled glasses and serve immediately. Serves 2.

pina colada

tropical rum blend

pimm's with ginger syrup

lychee and rum blast

long island iced tea

mint julep

opal ice   'citron' pressé

long island iced tea

30 ml (1 fl oz) vodka
30 ml (1 fl oz) gin
30 ml (1 fl oz) white rum
30 ml (1 fl oz) white tequila
30 ml (1 fl oz) Triple Sec
30 ml (1 fl oz) lemon juice
8 ice cubes
cola, to serve
lemon wedges, to garnish

Place the vodka, gin, rum, tequila, Triple Sec and lemon juice in a cocktail shaker with the ice and shake well. Pour into long, chilled glasses with ice, and add enough cola to colour the drink. Garnish with the lemon wedges. Serves 2.

mint julep

1 1/2 teaspoons caster (superfine) sugar
10 mint leaves
3/4 cup crushed ice
90 ml (3 fl oz) whisky
mint leaves, to garnish

Place the sugar, six of the mint leaves and a dash of water in a glass. Using a muddler or the end of a wooden spoon, mash the ingredients together until the sugar is dissolved and the mint is bruised. Fill the glass with crushed ice and top with the whisky. Stir well and place in the freezer for 30 minutes. Serve with a garnish of mint leaves and a straw. Serves 1.

opal ice

1 1/2 cups crushed ice
30 ml (1 fl oz) white rum
30 ml (1 fl oz) Triple Sec
30 ml (1 fl oz) Midori
1 tablespoon lime juice
1 tablespoon blue Curaçao

Divide the ice between two large cocktail glasses. Place the rum, Triple Sec, Midori and lime juice in a cocktail shaker, add a little ice and shake well. Pour three-quarters of the blend into the two glasses, then add the Curaçao. Top with the remaining cocktail mix. Serve immediately. Serves 2.

'citron' pressé

1/4 cup (2 fl oz) Absolut citron vodka
1/4 cup (2 fl oz) sugar syrup*
2 tablespoons lemon juice
ice, to fill cocktail shaker
lemon zest and peel, to garnish

Place all the ingredients except the ice and garnishes in a cocktail shaker. Shake well and pour into a highball glass containing some ice. Garnish with a generous grate of lemon zest and a twist of peel. Serves 1.

punch

2 cups (16 fl oz) peach nectar
200 ml (6 1/2 fl oz) dark rum
1/4 cup (2 fl oz) lime juice
3 white peaches, peeled and finely sliced
75 ml (2 1/2 fl oz) ginger syrup*
1 cup chopped fresh pineapple pieces
1 litre (32 fl oz) ginger beer or ginger wine
fresh lime and mint, to garnish

Place all of the ingredients except the garnishes into a large serving or punch bowl and stir well. Garnish with thinly sliced lime and torn mint leaves. Serves 8.

punch

tartlets with white bean purée and cherry tomatoes

salmon in pastry

artichoke tartlets

tartlets with white bean purée and cherry tomatoes

100 g (3½ oz) white beans, soaked overnight
2 cloves garlic
30 cherry tomatoes
1½ tablespoons fresh lemon thyme leaves
½ cup (4 fl oz) olive oil
30 pre-baked tart shells*

Drain the beans and place them with the garlic cloves in a saucepan filled with water. Bring to the boil and simmer for 30 minutes. Meanwhile, preheat the oven to 180°C (350°F) and place the tomatoes in a baking dish with 2 teaspoons of the lemon thyme leaves, ¼ cup (2 fl oz) of olive oil and ½ teaspoon of salt. Bake for 30 minutes. Add 2 teaspoons of salt to the white beans in the last 5 minutes of their cooking time. Check that the beans are soft, then drain. Mash by hand or in a food processor with the remaining olive oil and 1 tablespoon of thyme leaves. Season to taste with salt and freshly ground black pepper.
Fill each of the tart shells with a teaspoon of the white bean mash and top with one of the roasted cherry tomatoes. Serve immediately. Makes 30.

salmon in pastry

300 g (10 oz) salmon fillet, skin removed and boned
2 teaspoons sumac*
1 teaspoon grated fresh ginger
100 g (3½ oz) unsalted butter, cut into cubes
    and softened
1 tablespoon glacé ginger, finely chopped
1 tablespoon currants
1 kaffir lime leaf, finely sliced
2 sheets ready-prepared puff pastry, thawed
2 tablespoons milk

Preheat the oven to 200°C (400°F). Cut the salmon fillet lengthways into four 2 cm (¾ inch) wide strips. Place the sumac, ginger, softened butter, glacé ginger, currants and lime leaf in a bowl and mix until soft and well combined. Slice the pastry sheets in half and lie a piece of salmon along the centre of each one. Top each with a quarter of the flavoured butter and fold the pastry around the salmon, pressing the edges together at the top to form a seal. Place the salmon parcels on a baking tray lined with baking paper, ensure that the pastry is well sealed, and brush with a little milk. Bake for 20–25 minutes, or until golden brown. Remove and allow to cool until just warm. Slice into 2.5 cm (1 inch) portions and serve. Makes 30.

artichoke tartlets

120 g (4 oz) bottled artichoke hearts in oil, drained
15 cloves garlic, roasted until soft
¼ cup (2 fl oz) olive oil
½ teaspoon truffle oil
20 pre-baked tart shells*
30 g (1 oz) fresh parmesan cheese, shaved

Place the artichoke hearts, roasted garlic, olive oil and truffle oil in a blender or food processor and blend until smooth. Season according to taste with salt and freshly ground black pepper. Place 1 teaspoon of the mixture into each of the tart shells and top with the shaved parmesan. Makes 20.

smoked trout and pickled cucumber on oatcakes

oatcakes
2 cups fine oatmeal
½ teaspoon bicarbonate of soda (baking soda)
30 g (1 oz) butter, melted
oatmeal, extra, for rolling
smoked salmon topping
2 Lebanese cucumbers
2 tablespoons lemon juice
200 g (6½ oz) smoked trout, flaked
⅓ cup sour cream
1 tablespoon finely chopped lemon zest
3 teaspoons finely chopped fresh dill

Preheat the oven to 160°C (315°F). Mix the oatmeal, bicarbonate of soda and ½ teaspoon of salt together in a bowl. Add the melted butter and 150 ml (5 fl oz) of hot water. Stir well to form a soft dough. Sprinkle some oatmeal onto a clean work surface and knead gently for 1 minute. Divide the dough into four portions. Roll out one portion very thinly bewteen two sheets of baking paper. Using a 3–4 cm (1¼–1½ inch) round biscuit cutter, cut the dough into small rounds. Repeat with the remaining portions of dough. Place the rounds on a baking tray lined with baking paper and bake for 15–20 minutes, or until the oatcakes are pale and dry. Cool on a wire rack.
Slice the cucumbers in half lengthways and use a teaspoon to scoop out the seeds. Finely slice and sprinkle the flesh with 1 teaspoon of salt. Place in a sieve over a bowl and leave for 1 hour. Squeeze the cucumber of all liquid, then pat dry with paper towels. Place in a bowl, add 2 teaspoons of the lemon juice and mix well. In another bowl, combine the trout, sour cream and lemon zest. Season with salt and freshly ground black pepper and add the remaining lemon juice, tasting as you go. Place a teaspoon of the trout mixture onto each of the oatcakes and top with a little of the cucumber. Sprinkle with dill and serve. Makes 24.

smoked trout and pickled cucumber on oatcakes

seared beef with roasted tomato salsa

500 g (1 lb) Roma (egg) tomatoes, quartered
1 teaspoon sugar
10 basil leaves, shredded
10 mint leaves, shredded
1 teaspoon balsamic vinegar
300 g (10 oz) beef fillet, about 4 cm (1½ inches) in diameter
1 tablespoon vegetable oil
1 baguette (French bread stick), sliced thinly, to serve

Preheat the oven to 160°C (315°F). Place the tomato quarters in a baking dish and sprinkle with the sugar and 1 teaspoon of salt. Bake for 40 minutes, or until the tomatoes begin to blacken at the edges and dry out. Remove from the heat and allow to cool. Slice the roasted tomatoes thinly and place in a bowl with the shredded basil and mint leaves. Add the balsamic vinegar and mix well to combine. Season the beef fillet with freshly ground black pepper. Heat the oil in a frying pan over high heat and sear the fillet for 2 minutes on all sides. Remove from the heat and sprinkle with a little sea salt. Set aside to cool, then slice into 1 cm (½ inch) widths. Place on the baguette slices and top with a little of the tomato salsa. Makes 30.

sweet potato crisps with babaghannouj

2 tablespoons olive oil
1 head of garlic, sliced in half horizontally
1 large eggplant (aubergine)
⅓ cup tahini*
¼ cup (2 fl oz) lemon juice
¼ cup finely chopped fresh flat-leaf (Italian) parsley
1 large sweet potato
2 cups (16 fl oz) vegetable oil
1 teaspoon sumac*

Preheat the oven to 200°C (400°F). Place the olive oil in a baking dish. Place each garlic half, cut-side down, on the dish, and add the whole eggplant. Bake for 35–40 minutes, or until the cloves are golden brown and the eggplant is soft. Remove from the oven and allow to cool, then remove the flesh from the roasted garlic and place it in a blender or food processor. Cut the eggplant in half, scoop out the flesh and add it to the garlic. Blend until smooth. Transfer to a bowl and fold in the tahini. Add the lemon juice, and add salt according to taste. Fold through the parsley and set aside. Slice the sweet potato very thinly with a sharp knife or vegetable peeler. Heat the oil in a deep frying pan over moderate heat and deep-fry the sweet potato, a few pieces at a time, until they are crisp and golden. Drain on paper towels. Sprinkle with sumac and sea salt and serve with a heaped teaspoon of the eggplant mixture. Serves 6.

fig roll with pecorino

250 g (8 oz) dried figs, chopped into very small pieces
2½ teaspoons redcurrant jelly
1 teaspoon brandy
¼ cup chopped walnut pieces
¼ teaspoon aniseed seeds
6–8 sheets rice paper*
50 g (1¾ oz) pecorino cheese, thinly sliced, to serve

Place all the ingredients except the rice paper and pecorino cheese in a food processor and pulse until the mixture begins to clump together. Transfer to baking paper and form into a roll. Wrap in rice paper and leave, uncovered, for 3–4 days. Slice and serve with slices of pecorino cheese. Makes 40 slices.

eggplant rounds with sweet harissa and mint

4 small or Japanese eggplants (aubergines)
150 ml (5 fl oz) vegetable oil
2 red capsicums (peppers), roasted, skins removed
2 teaspoons roasted ground cumin
2 teaspoons roasted ground coriander
2 small red chillies, seeded and finely chopped
½ teaspoon paprika
½ cup roughly chopped fresh flat-leaf (Italian) parsley
1 cup roughly chopped fresh coriander (cilantro) leaves
2 cloves garlic
3 tablespoons olive oil
6 mint leaves
½ teaspoon brown sugar
24 mint leaves, extra, to serve

Trim the ends off the eggplants and cut them into 2 cm (¾ inch) discs. Place in a colander over a bowl and lightly salt. Allow to sit for 20–30 minutes before rinsing and squeezing dry. Heat the oil in a deep frying pan over moderate heat and cook the eggplant rounds in batches until golden, turning once. Drain on paper towels. Make the harissa by placing the roasted capsicum, cumin, coriander, chilli, paprika, parsley, fresh coriander, garlic, olive oil, mint leaves, sugar and 1 teaspoon of salt in a blender and blending to form a smooth paste. Place ½ teaspoon amounts of harissa onto each of the eggplant rounds, top with a fresh mint leaf and serve. Makes 24. note – This mix makes more harissa than you need, but it will keep in the refrigerator in a sealed container for 5 days and is a good, spicy stand-by for grilled fish, chicken or roasted vegetables.

seared beef with roasted tomato salsa

fig roll with pecorino

sweet potato crisps with babaghannouj

eggplant rounds with sweet harissa and mint

WHISKY SOUR Three-quarters fill a cocktail shaker with ice. Add 1/4 cup (2 fl oz) of whisky, 30 ml (1 fl oz) of lemon juice, 1 teaspoon of caster (superfine) sugar and a dash of egg white. Shake well. Strain into a small cocktail glass containing ice and a maraschino cherry. Serves 1.

GIN FIZZ Into a cocktail shaker filled with ice, place 1/4 cup (2 fl oz) of gin, 1 tablespoon of lemon juice, 1 teaspoon of caster (superfine) sugar and a dash of egg white. Shake vigorously and pour into a chilled glass. Top with soda water. Serves 1.

GREYHOUND Place ¼ cup (2 fl oz) of vodka, 100 ml (3½ fl oz) of freshly squeezed grapefruit juice and a dash of either Cointreau or Triple Sec into a tall glass. Stir, then top with ice. Serves 1. This drink is also suitable to serve in a large jug. Increase the quantity accordingly.

NEGRONI Fill two chilled glasses with ice and add 30 ml (1 fl oz) of Campari, 30 ml (1 fl oz) of sweet vermouth and 30 ml (1 fl oz) of gin. Lightly stir the mixture to 'marble' the different coloured alcohols, and garnish with slices of orange peel. Serves 1.

ceviche with coconut dressing

tuna and red pepper skewers

squid stuffed with lemon risotto

ceviche with coconut dressing

500 g (1 lb) firm white-fleshed fish, skin removed and boned
3 limes, juiced
100 ml (3¹/₂ fl oz) coconut cream
1 teaspoon grated fresh ginger
¹/₂ teaspoon turmeric
1 teaspoon sugar
1 tablespoon finely chopped fresh coriander (cilantro) root
2 spring (green) onions, finely sliced on the diagonal

Slice the fish into bite-sized pieces and place in a glass or ceramic dish. Cover with the lime juice and refrigerate for 2 hours. Place the coconut cream, ginger, turmeric, sugar, coriander root and ¹/₂ teaspoon of salt in a bowl and stir to combine. Drain the fish and add to the coconut dressing. Sprinkle with the spring onion and serve. Makes 40 serves.

tuna and red pepper skewers

500 g (1 lb) tuna fillet
1 tablespoon olive oil
1 teaspoon ground coriander
2 teaspoons ground cumin
¹/₂ cup (4 fl oz) lemon mayonnaise*
1 tablespoon finely chopped preserved lemon
1 tablespoon finely chopped fresh coriander
   (cilantro) leaves
2 tablespoons lime juice
1 red capsicum (pepper)
20 small skewers, soaked in hot water
   for 20 minutes

Cut the tuna into 2 cm (³/₄ inch) cubes and place in a bowl. Add the oil, ground coriander and cumin and mix through. Set aside and allow to marinate for 1 hour. Preheat the oven to 180°C (350°F). Place the mayonnaise in a small bowl and stir in the preserved lemon, coriander leaves and lime juice. Slice the capsicum into 2 cm (³/₄ inch) squares and then skewer on two alternate pieces of tuna and capsicum per skewer. Place on a baking tray and bake for 5–7 minutes. Season with salt and freshly ground black pepper and serve with the mayonnaise. Makes 20.

squid stuffed with lemon risotto

750 ml (24 fl oz) fish or vegetable stock
30 g (1 oz) butter
1 cup finely diced brown onion
1 clove garlic, crushed
1 teaspoon fresh thyme leaves
1 cup Arborio (risotto) rice
3 teaspoons finely chopped lemon zest
2 tablespoons lemon juice
¹/₂ cup roughly chopped fresh flat-leaf (Italian) parsley
6 medium squid, each approximately 15 cm (6 inches) long

Preheat the oven to 180°C (350°F). Heat the stock in a saucepan and keep at a low simmer. Melt the butter in a medium-sized saucepan over moderate heat and cook the onion, garlic and thyme, stirring occasionally, for 5–7 minutes, or until the onion is transparent. Add the rice and zest and stir well until coated. Add ¹/₂ cup (4 fl oz) of hot stock and stir constantly over medium heat until all the liquid has been absorbed. Continue adding more liquid, half a cup at a time, until all the liquid has been absorbed and the rice is creamy and tender. Remove from the heat and add the lemon juice, parsley, salt and freshly ground black pepper.
Clean the squid, removing the tentacles from the body. Stuff the body with the risotto and place in a baking dish with ¹/₂ cup (4 fl oz) of water or stock. Cover with foil and bake for 30 minutes. Remove and allow to cool a little before slicing at 2 cm (³/₄ inch) intervals. Makes 24 slices.

pickled nectarines with ricotta and prosciutto

3 large nectarines (approximately 500 g / 1 lb)
150 ml (5 fl oz) cider vinegar
2 star anise
2 cloves
1 teaspoon roughly sliced fresh ginger
1 large fresh red chilli
1 cup caster (superfine) sugar
12 slices prosciutto*, cut in half lengthways
250 g (8 oz) ricotta cheese

Slice the nectarines into quarters. Place the vinegar, star anise, cloves, ginger, chilli, sugar, 1 teaspoon of salt and 300 ml (10 fl oz) of water in a saucepan and bring to the boil. Warm a medium-sized, heatproof, sealable jar by filling it with boiling water, waiting a few minutes and then draining the water. Place the nectarines in the jar, pour in the boiling vinegar liquid and seal. Cool, then place in the refrigerator for at least 5 days. Slice the nectarine quarters in half. To serve, lay the prosciutto slices out on a clean surface and lay one slice of nectarine on top of each. Top with a heaped teaspoon of ricotta and roll up. Makes 24.

pickled nectarines with ricotta and prosciutto

soy beef fillet with pickled ginger   chilli hushpuppies

prawn and water chestnut wontons with plum sauce

crab with lemon, parsley and chilli

soy beef fillet with pickled ginger

300 g (10 oz) beef fillet
3 tablespoons soy sauce
3 tablespoons mirin*
1 tablespoon vegetable oil
1 cup shredded daikon*
1/2 cup shredded cucumber
1 teaspoon grated fresh ginger
1 teaspoon sesame oil
1 nori sheet*
2 tablespoons pickled ginger*

Cut the beef fillet in half lengthways. Place 2 tablespoons each of the soy sauce and mirin into a ceramic dish, add the beef fillets, cover and marinate in the fridge overnight, turning the beef occasionally.
Heat the oil in a frying pan over high heat and sear the beef for several minutes on each side. Season with sea salt and freshly ground black pepper, cover with foil and allow to cool. Place the daikon, cucumber, fresh ginger, sesame oil and the remaining tablespoon each of soy sauce and mirin in a bowl and toss together. Slice the nori sheet into 2 cm (3/4 inch) wide strips and then cut each strip in half.
Slice the beef very thinly. Place a little of the daikon salad and a small piece of pickled ginger onto one of the beef slices and roll it up. Place it onto a strip of nori and roll again. Place the parcel onto a plate with the loose end of the nori facing down. Repeat with the remaining ingredients. Serve at room temperature. Makes 15–20.

chilli hushpuppies

3/4 cup plain (all-purpose) flour
1 teaspoon baking powder
1 egg
20 g (3/4 oz) butter, melted
1/4 cup (2 fl oz) milk
1 teaspoon Tabasco sauce
2 fresh corn cobs, kernels removed
   (approximately 2 cups)
100 ml (3 1/2 fl oz) vegetable oil

Place the flour, baking powder, egg, melted butter and 1/2 teaspoon of salt in a mixing bowl and stir together. Add the milk and Tabasco sauce to form a thick batter, then add the fresh corn. Heat the oil over medium heat. Drop small spoonfuls of the batter into the oil and fry each side until golden brown. Remove and drain on paper towels. Serve while still warm. Makes 20.

prawn and water chestnut wontons with plum sauce

450 g green (raw) prawns, or 210 g (7 oz)
   prawn meat, chopped
1/2 cup finely diced water chestnuts
1/2 cup finely sliced spring (green) onions
2 tablespoons mirin*
1/2 teaspoon sesame oil
2 teaspoons fish sauce
1 egg
30 round wonton wrappers*
peanut (groundnut) oil, for deep-frying
plum sauce*

Place the prawn meat, water chestnuts, spring onions, mirin, sesame oil, fish sauce, 1 teaspoon of sea salt and some ground black pepper in a bowl and stir to combine. Beat the egg in a small bowl with 1/4 cup (2 fl oz) of water. Place one of the wonton wrappers onto a clean surface and place 1 teaspoon of the prawn mixture at its centre. Brush a little of the egg wash around the edges and bring together, sealing the sides, and twist the top firmly.
Place on a tray lined with baking paper and repeat with the remaining mixture.
Heat the oil in a wok or deep frying pan and fry the wontons until they are golden brown. Remove and serve with plum sauce. Serves 36.

crab with lemon, parsley and chilli

10 slices white bread, crusts removed
50 ml (1 3/4 fl oz) olive oil
250 g (8 oz) crab meat, shredded
2 tablespoons grated lemon rind
1 tablespoon virgin olive oil
1 small red chilli, seeded and finely chopped
1/3 cup finely chopped fresh flat-leaf
   (Italian) parsley
2 teaspoons lemon juice

Preheat the oven to 160°C (315°F). Cut each slice of bread into four circles using a biscuit cutter. Place on an oven tray, lightly brush with olive oil and bake until golden brown. Allow to cool. Place the crab meat in a medium-sized bowl, add the remaining ingredients and stir well to combine. Place a heaped teaspoon of the crab mix onto each of the little toasts and serve immediately. Makes 40.
note – This mix will keep well for several hours, so it is an easy one to prepare in advance.

rhubarb, strawberry and white rum chiller

berry ice

mexican shot

sorbet vodka shot

rhubarb, strawberry and white rum chiller

1/2 cup stewed rhubarb*
6 strawberries
1/4 cup (2 fl oz) white rum
1 teaspoon vanilla essence
8 ice cubes
strawberries, to garnish

Place all the ingredients except the garnish in a blender and blend until smooth. Pour into chilled glasses and garnish with a small strawberry. Serves 2.

berry ice

6 strawberries
1/2 cup frozen blackberries
1/4 cup (2 fl oz) sugar syrup*
1/4 cup (2 fl oz) vodka
10 ice cubes

Place the strawberries, blackberries, sugar syrup, vodka and ice in a blender and blend to form an icy slush. Pour into cocktail glasses and serve immediately. Serves 2.

mexican shot

90 ml (3 fl oz) tequila
90 ml (3 fl oz) tomato juice
1 cup roughly chopped Roma (egg) tomatoes
1 tablespoon chilli syrup*
1 teaspoon lime juice
1 tomato, extra, finely diced
2 tablespoons finely chopped fresh coriander
   (cilantro) leaves

Place the tequila, tomato juice, chopped tomato, chilli syrup and lime juice in a blender and blend until smooth. Pour into a small container and fold in the diced tomato and coriander. Place in the freezer for several hours or overnight. Break up with a fork, or place in a blender and pulse. Spoon into cocktail glasses and serve immediately. Serves 6.

sorbet vodka shot

6 tablespoons fruit sorbet
1/2 cup (4 fl oz) vodka

Divide the fruit sorbet between six chilled shot glasses and pour a tablespoon of vodka over each. Serves 6.

ripe cherry

1/4 cup (2 fl oz) Framboise
30 ml (1 fl oz) Malibu
30 ml (1 fl oz) white crème de cacao
crushed ice, to serve

Place all the ingredients except the ice in a cocktail shaker and shake well. Pour over crushed ice and serve immediately. Serves 2.

ripe cherry

salt and pepper tofu

welsh rarebit

walnut crisps with creamed goat's cheese and pear

salt and pepper tofu

1 egg white
2 cloves garlic, crushed
1 teaspoon grated fresh ginger
500 g (1 lb) firm tofu, cut into 2 cm (³/4 inch) cubes
3 tablespoons sugar
2 teaspoons lime juice
1 teaspoon finely chopped red chilli
¼ cup finely diced cucumber
2 tablespoons finely chopped fresh coriander (cilantro) leaves
½ cup cornflour (cornstarch)
1 tablespoon ground Szechwan peppercorns
1 teaspoon caster (superfine) sugar
1 small red chilli, extra, seeded and finely chopped
300 ml (10 fl oz) peanut (groundnut) oil, for frying
1 tablespoon finely chopped fresh coriander
   (cilantro) leaves, extra, to serve

Lightly whisk the egg white, then add the garlic, ginger and tofu. Stir to coat the tofu, then cover and refrigerate overnight. To make a cucumber sauce, place the sugar and ¹/3 cup (2³/4 fl oz) of water in a small saucepan and bring to the boil. Cool, add the lime, chilli, cucumber and coriander. Set aside. In a shallow bowl, mix together the cornflour, Szechwan pepper, sugar, chilli, 1 tablespoon of sea salt and 1 teaspoon each of freshly ground white pepper and black pepper. Heat the oil in a deep frying pan or saucepan over moderate heat. Coat the tofu in the flour mixture, shake off any excess and deep-fry in batches for about 1 minute, or until the tofu is lightly coloured. Drain on paper towels. Repeat with the remaining tofu. Serve immediately, sprinkled with coriander and accompanied by the cucumber sauce. Serves 6–8.

welsh rarebit

30 g (1 oz) butter
2 tablespoons plain (all-purpose) flour
2 teaspoons wholegrain mustard
½ cup (4 fl oz) Guinness or stout
½ teaspoon Worcestershire sauce
150 g (5 oz) mature cheddar, grated
9 slices white bread, crusts removed and lightly toasted

Preheat the oven to 180°C (350°F). Melt the butter in a small saucepan over medium heat and stir in the flour. Add 1 teaspoon of salt, some freshly ground black pepper and the mustard, and continue to stir until the mixture begins to turn golden brown. Add the Guinness and Worcestershire sauce and whisk until the mixture is smooth and quite thick. Add three-quarters of the grated cheese and continue to whisk until the cheese has melted. Spread thickly onto the pieces of toast and sprinkle with the remaining cheese. Place in the oven for 10 minutes. Remove and slice into squares. Serve while warm. Makes 36 small squares.

walnut crisps with creamed goat's cheese and pear

1 teaspoon dry yeast powder
1 teaspoon sugar
1½ cups plain (all-purpose) flour
30 g (1 oz) finely chopped walnuts
1 tablespoon walnut oil
150 g (5 oz) fresh goat's cheese
½ cup (4 fl oz) cream
2 ripe pears

Mix the yeast, sugar and ½ cup (4 fl oz) of warm water in a small bowl. Cover and leave in a warm place for 10 minutes or until frothy. Place the flour, walnuts and ¼ teaspoon of salt in a bowl, make a well in the centre and add the yeast mixture. Mix to form a dough, gather into a ball, then turn out onto a lightly floured surface and knead until smooth. Transfer to a large bowl brushed with walnut oil, cover and leave in a warm place for 1 hour, or until doubled in size. Punch down, halve the mixture and shape each portion into a sausage shape approximately 23 cm long x 3 cm thick (9 inches x 1 1/4 inches). Twist each sausage to form a loose spiral and place on a greased baking tray. Cover and leave in a warm place for 40 minutes, or until doubled in size. Preheat the oven to 180°C (350°F). Bake the loaves for 25–30 minutes, or until golden and hollow-sounding when tapped. Cool on a wire rack. Slice each walnut loaf into 5 mm (1/4 inch) slices, cutting on a diagonal. Reduce the oven temperature to 160°C (315°F). Place the slices on a flat baking tray and return to the oven for 8–10 minutes, or until slightly coloured and crisp. Allow to cool on wire racks. Mix the goat's cheese and cream together, and season with salt and freshly ground black pepper. To assemble, spread a small amount of the goat's cheese mixture on top of each slice of walnut bread. Cut the pears into thin wedges and place on top of the goat's cheese. Makes 50.

watermelon squares

½ large seedless watermelon
50 g (1³/4 oz) feta
1 teaspoon sumac*
6 black olives, seeded and finely sliced
1½ tablespoons finely chopped fresh flat-leaf (Italian) parsley
1 teaspoon finely chopped fresh thyme leaves

Cut the watermelon flesh into 3 cm (1 1/4 inch) cubes. Using a melon baller, remove a scoop of watermelon from the top of each cube. Set the cubes aside. Cut the feta into 1 cm (½ inch) cubes and place a piece into the top of each of the watermelon cubes. Toss the sumac, sliced olives, parsley and thyme together in a small bowl, then place a small amount on top of each of the feta squares. Serve immediately. Makes approximately 25.

watermelon squares

basics

sweet finale

Finish an evening on a sweet note. At the end of a party, as a post-theatre entertainment, or just as an indulgent way to entertain friends, small trays of desserts and coffee shots are a graceful way to express the winding down of the day.

hot drinks

Coffee at the end of the day should ideally be short, rich and sweet. Add a little vanilla to the coffee, or place a few cardamom pods in the pot or cup for a sweet, spicy finish. Since not everyone likes to drink coffee at night, always have a selection of herbal teas on hand, or fill glasses with fresh mint, lemon grass or ginger for a lightly infused tea.

winter warmers

Winter warming doesn't get any easier than with a selection of rich liqueurs and sweet fruit. Dip ripe figs into Grand Marnier, or slivers of pear into Frangelico. An old favourite and an ideal alternative to after-dinner drinks in winter is a large jug of warmed and spiced mulled wine. It's ideally served with gingerbread, spiced biscotti and a bowl of liqueur-laced crème fraîche*.

waterworks

Ensure that your guests maintain their water intake by always having on hand jugs of chilled water. Flavour the water with fresh lemon or a little lemon syrup, a dash of orange flower water* or a sprinkle of rosewater*.

edible gold

Add exoticism to your desserts with the glimmer of gold and silver. Edible gold and silver leaf are available from most cake-decorating or Indian speciality shops. Peel the leaf carefully from its backing paper by one corner, ensuring that you touch the sheet as little as possible to avoid having it dissolve in your hand. Layer the leaf over chocolate brownies, fold it through jelly, or blend it into late-night spirits.

a mellow mood

Contrary to club-land opinion, late nights should be all about soft lighting and a languorous tempo. Set the scene with dozens of tea-lights, piles of soft cushions, your favourite smooth tunes and richly scented flowers.

a mellow mood

waterworks

hot drinks

edible gold

winter warmers

good ideas

refreshing fruit

Sometimes all you need at the end of the night is fresh fruit: big bowls of cherries, strawberries piled high, chilled wedges of watermelon and pineapple, or for a kitsch twist, drunken melon balls.

coffee shots

While some people like their coffee unadulterated, it is nice to be able to offer a few sweet options. Fill small coffee glasses with chocolate, vanilla or hazelnut gelato and simply add a shot of espresso.

chocolate berries

Melt 50 g (1 3/4 oz) of white chocolate with 100 ml (3 1/2 fl oz) of cream. Add a sprinkle of cinnamon and 1–2 tablespoons of white crème de cacao. Stir to combine. Allow to cool, then pour over berries.

sweet treats

When time is limited, buy it in. Pile a plate with nougat, fudge, Turkish delight and peanut brittle and let everyone choose a favourite.

fruit sorbets

Buy a selection of fruit sorbets and serve tiny scoops in small, chilled glasses with a dash of raspberry purée or fresh passionfruit pulp.

smashed chocolate

Indulge in a large block of high-quality chocolate and use a sharp knife to shatter it into bite-sized pieces. Pile the pieces onto a platter and serve alongside dried muscatel grapes.

little twists

If you have a favourite dessert, why not make a smaller version of it? Try tiny pavlovas, individual pots of lemon delicious, Chinese spoons of crème brûlée or sugared squares of bread-and-butter pudding.

quince and rosewater tarts   fresh fig tarts

strawberry rice pudding

quince and rosewater tarts

90 g (3 oz) quince paste*
1/3 cup (2 3/4 fl oz) orange juice
120 g (4 oz) mascarpone*
1/2 teaspoon rosewater*
2 teaspoons icing (confectioners') sugar
1 tablespoon almond meal, lightly toasted
12 pre-baked tart shells*

Melt the quince paste with the orange juice in a bowl over a saucepan of simmering water. Stir well to combine, then remove and allow to cool.
Blend the mascarpone with the rosewater, icing sugar and almond meal. Spoon the mascarpone mixture into the tart shells and top with the cooled quince paste. Makes 12.

fresh fig tarts

1/4 cup honey
120 g (4 oz) mascarpone*
12 pre-baked tart shells*
3 fresh figs, thinly sliced
1/3 cup roughly chopped toasted hazelnuts
1 tablespoon icing (confectioners') sugar

Place the honey and mascarpone in a bowl and blend with a spoon until the mixture is smooth. Spoon into the tart shells and top with the thinly sliced fresh fig and a scatter of hazelnuts. Sprinkle with icing sugar and serve. Makes 12.

strawberry rice pudding

2 cups (16 fl oz) milk
1/4 cup sugar
2 teaspoons finely chopped orange zest
3 cardamom pods
1/3 cup short-grain rice
1/2 cup (4 fl oz) cream, whipped
60 g (2 oz) pistachios, crushed
300 g (10 oz) strawberries

Bring the milk to the boil with the sugar, orange zest, cardamom pods and a pinch of salt, then tip in the rice. Reduce the heat and simmer gently for 30 minutes, or until the rice is cooked. Remove the cardamom pods. Allow the rice to cool, then fold in the cream with half of the pistachios. Layer rice and strawberries into small glass bowls, starting with the rice, then fruit, and so on. Top with a sprinkle of the remaining pistachios. Makes 10 small bowls, or 6 regular serves.

marinated raspberries with coconut ice

1/4 cup (2 fl oz) orange juice
1 tablespoon Grand Marnier (optional)
400 g (13 oz) raspberries
1/4 cup (2 fl oz) milk
1/2 cup sugar
1/2 cup icing (confectioners') sugar
1/2 cup desiccated coconut
10 g (1/4 oz) butter
1/2 teaspoon orange flower water*
2 drops pink food colouring (cochineal)

Combine the orange juice and Grand Marnier in a small bowl, very gently stir in the raspberries and leave for 30 minutes to marinate.
Bring the milk and sugars to the boil and boil gently for 3 minutes. Add the coconut and butter and boil for 1 minute, then add the orange flower water and pink food colouring. Take off the heat and stir until the mixture resembles breadcrumbs. Store in an airtight container until ready to use. Pile the raspberries into small glasses or bowls and sprinkle with the coconut ice. Makes 10 small serves or 4 regular serves.

marinated raspberries with coconut ice

CLASSIC RUSTY NAIL Place 30 ml (1 fl oz) of whisky, 30 ml (1 fl oz) of Drambuie and 3 ice cubes into a chilled glass. Stir well to combine. Serves 1. The rusty nail is the perfect drink for a late winter's night, and can be served with or without ice, according to taste.

BRANDY ALEXANDER Place 50 ml (1 3/4 fl oz) of brandy, 30 ml (1 fl oz) of crème de cacao, 1 tablespoon of cream and 3–4 ice cubes in a cocktail shaker and shake vigorously several times. Pour into a cocktail glass and garnish with a sprinkle of nutmeg. Serves 1.

PEACH TREE Fill a small tumbler with ice and pour over ¼ cup (2 fl oz) of peach syrup and ¼ cup (2 fl oz) of dark Jamaican rum. Stir well and garnish with a wedge of lime. Serves 1. The syrup from poached summer fruit makes an ideal base for this drink.

SOUR CHERRY BLOSSOM Into a shaker half-filled with ice, place 1 tablespoon of cream, ¼ cup (2 fl oz) of gin, ¼ cup (2 fl oz) of sour cherry nectar*, 1 egg white and 1 tablespoon of framboise. Shake vigorously and pour into small, chilled cocktail glasses. Serves 2.

ice cream trifles with turkish delight

fig surprise   chocolate caramel 'brûlées'

ice cream trifles with turkish delight

250 g (8 oz) raspberries or strawberries
6 cubes Turkish delight*
12 plain chocolate biscuits
2 cups vanilla ice cream, scooped
1/2 cup blanched almonds, toasted

Purée the berries to form a sauce and set aside. Cut the Turkish delight into eighths so as to make small cubes. Break the biscuits into small pieces and set aside. Layer the ice cream, chocolate biscuits, Turkish delight and blanched almonds into six chilled glasses and top with the berry sauce. Serve immediately. Serves 6.

fig surprise

3 fresh figs
2 teaspoons finely chopped glacé ginger
2 tablespoons brown sugar
1/4 teaspoon grated lemon rind
1/4 teaspoon ground cinnamon
3 sheets ready-prepared filo pastry
50 g (1 3/4 oz) unsalted butter, melted
icing (confectioners') sugar, to serve
vanilla or honey ice cream, to serve

Preheat the oven to 200°C (400°F). Cut each fig into eight wedges. In a small bowl, combine the glacé ginger, brown sugar, lemon rind and cinnamon. Stir to combine. Cut each sheet of filo into eight equal portions. Take one sheet and lightly brush it with the melted butter. Place a piece of fig against the side so that the stem end is outside the pastry. Place a little of the brown sugar mixture onto the fig and then fold the filo around the fig, leaving the stem section free. Repeat with the other pieces of pastry and place the wrapped figs onto a baking tray lined with baking paper. Bake for 7–10 minutes, or until golden brown. Cool on a wire rack. Sprinkle with icing sugar and serve warm with vanilla or honey ice cream. Makes 24.

chocolate caramel 'brûlées'

1 1/2 cups (12 fl oz) cream
1 cup (8 fl oz) milk
1 vanilla bean, split and scraped
5 egg yolks
3/4 cup sugar
30 g (1 oz) dark chocolate, grated
Dutch cocoa powder, to serve

Preheat the oven to 150°C (300°F). Place the cream, milk and vanilla bean in a saucepan and heat until almost boiling. Remove from the heat. In a large bowl, beat the egg yolks with 1/4 cup of the sugar and a pinch of salt until thick and pale. Place the remaining sugar in a heavy-based saucepan and melt it over medium heat. When it has become a golden brown colour, pour over the hot milk and whisk until the toffeed sugar has dissolved. Pour this hot mixture over the egg mix and whisk to combine. Strain and pour into ten 100 ml (3 1/2 fl oz) capacity ramekins. Place them in a baking dish and fill the dish with hot water until the water comes two-thirds of the way up the side of the pots. Cover with foil and bake for 20–25 minutes. Remove from the oven and take off the foil. Sprinkle the grated chocolate over the top of the custards until the surface is completely covered. Wipe the edges of the pots clean. Allow to cool before serving. Serve sprinkled with cocoa powder. Serves 10.

schnapps jellies

1 cup sugar
1 cinnamon stick
2 star anise
4 strips lemon peel
2 cups (16 fl oz) apple schnapps
12 leaves gelatine
3 sheets edible silver leaf*

Place 2 cups (16 fl oz) of water in a small saucepan with the sugar, cinnamon, star anise and lemon peel. Bring to the boil, stirring to dissolve the sugar. Reduce the heat and allow the syrup to simmer for 10 minutes. Cool slightly, strain the syrup into a bowl and add the schnapps. Place the gelatine sheets into a bowl of cold water and leave them to soften for 5 minutes. Squeeze the gelatine of any excess water and place it into the bowl of warm schnapps. Stir until the gelatine has dissolved, then pour the liquid into a 20 x 30 cm (8 x 12 inch) tray lined with plastic wrap. Lay the sheets of silver leaf over the surface of the jelly. Chill for several hours or overnight, then cut into squares to serve. Makes 25 squares.

schnapps jellies

spiced biscotti with marsala mascarpone

tiny tiramisu

ice cream shots with sweet liqueurs

ice cream with wafers

spiced biscotti with marsala mascarpone

2 cups plain (all-purpose) flour
1 cup caster (superfine) sugar
2 teaspoons baking powder
100 g (3½ oz) dried figs, sliced
50 g (1¾ oz) dried apricots, sliced
150 g (5 oz) slivered almonds
2 teaspoons chopped lemon zest
¼ teaspoon ground cardamom
1 teaspoon ground cinnamon
3 eggs, beaten
200 g (6½ oz) mascarpone*
2 tablespoons sweet Marsala
1 tablespoon caster (superfine) sugar, extra,

Preheat the oven to 180°C (350°F). Mix the flour, sugar, baking powder, dried fruit, almonds, lemon zest, cardamom and cinnamon in a large bowl and make a well in the centre. Fold in the eggs to make a sticky dough. Divide into four pieces and roll out each portion of dough to form logs 4 cm (1½ inches) in diameter. Place the logs on a baking tray lined with baking paper, leaving space between each log to spread a little, and bake for 30 minutes. Remove and allow to cool. Reduce the oven temperature to 140°C (275°F). With a sharp bread knife, cut each of the loaves into thin slices approximately 5 mm (¼ inch) wide. Lay the biscuits on a baking tray and return them to the oven. Bake for 20 minutes, turning the biscuits once. Remove from the oven and cool on wire racks.
Place the mascarpone, Marsala and caster sugar in a small bowl and mix until smooth. Serve the biscotti accompanied with the mascarpone. Makes approximately 120 biscuits.

ice cream shots with sweet liqueurs

12 small scoops hazelnut ice cream
60 g (2 oz) dark chocolate, grated
100 ml (3½ fl oz) Frangelico

Divide the ice cream and chocolate among six small glasses and top with the liqueur. Serves 6.
note – You can play around with any number of ice cream and liqueur combinations: for example, chocolate ice cream with Tia Maria, coffee ice cream with crème de cacao, or vanilla ice cream with Grand Marnier.

tiny tiramisu

coffee syrup
2 tablespoons sugar
½ cup (4 fl oz) strong black coffee
½ cup (4 fl oz) Tia Maria
coffee cupcakes
¼ cup (2 fl oz) strong black coffee
2 eggs
100 g (3½ oz) unsalted butter, softened
¾ cup sugar
1½ cups plain (all-purpose) flour
2 teaspoons baking powder
¼ cup almond meal
mascarpone filling
1 tablespoon sugar
2 egg yolks
½ cup (4 fl oz) Marsala
250 g (8 oz) mascarpone*
¼ cup (2 fl oz) unsweetened cocoa powder, for dusting

Make a coffee syrup by bringing the sugar and coffee to the boil in a small saucepan. Simmer for 5 minutes. Remove, allow to cool, then stir through the Tia Maria. To make the cupcakes, preheat the oven to 180°C (350°F). Place all the cupcake ingredients in a food processor and blend until smooth. Spoon tablespoons of the mixture into patty cake tins and bake for 12 minutes. Cool on wire racks. Make the filling by placing the sugar, egg yolks and Marsala in a bowl over a saucepan of simmering water and whisking until frothy. Remove and chill. Fold through the mascarpone. With a small knife, remove the lids from the cakes, cutting a well in the centre. Spoon a tablespoon of coffee syrup, then a tablespoon of the mascarpone, into the top of each cake. Replace the tops of the cakes and dust with cocoa powder. Allow to sit for several hours before serving. Makes 24.

ice cream with wafers

⅓ cup desiccated coconut
¼ cup caster (superfine) sugar
1 teaspoon plain (all-purpose) flour
¼ teaspoon baking powder
40 g (1¼ oz) unsalted butter, melted
1 egg white
500 ml (16 fl oz) vanilla ice cream

Preheat the oven to 160°C (315°F). Combine the coconut, sugar, flour and baking powder in a bowl. Stir in the melted butter, then add the egg white and whisk until smooth. Line a baking tray with baking paper and spread a tablespoon of the batter thinly over the surface. Bake for 7 minutes, or until pale gold. Cool slightly, then cut into squares. Repeat until all the wafers have been cooked. Sandwich a slice of ice cream between two wafers. Serve immediately. Makes 5.

hot chocolate

hot toddy

smooth sambucca

hangover cure

hot chocolate

200 ml (6¹/2 fl oz) milk
60 g (2 oz) dark chocolate, grated
4 tablespoons Frangelico

Place the milk and grated chocolate in a small saucepan over low heat and cook, stirring occasionally, until the chocolate has melted. Pour into four shot or cocktail glasses and top each with a tablespoon of Frangelico. Serve immediately. Serves 4.
note – Any sweet liqueur will suit this recipe, so choose your favourite: for example, Malibu, drambuie, Grand Marnier, crème de cacao or Tia Maria.

hot toddy

1/2 teaspoon brown sugar
1 strip lemon peel
1 clove
1 cinnamon stick
1/4 cup (2 fl oz) whisky

Place all the ingredients into a glass and top with boiling water. Serves 1.

smooth sambucca

30 ml (1 fl oz) crème de cacao
30 ml (1 fl oz) Sambucca

Pour the crème de cacao into a shot glass and then add the Sambucca, pouring it over the back of a spoon so that the liqueurs form two distinct layers. Serves 1.

hangover cure

1/4 cup (2 fl oz) Fernet-Branca
30 ml (1 fl oz) Vermouth Rosso
1 tablespoon crème de menthe
ice, to serve

Pour the three liqueurs over ice, mix well and serve. Serves 1.

chilled knight

2 cups (16 fl oz) Vermouth Rosso
1 tablespoon Fernet-Branca
1/2 cup seedless raisins
rind of 2 oranges
5 cardamom pods, crushed
6 cloves
1 tablespoon grated fresh ginger
2 cinnamon sticks
300 g (10 oz) sugar
1.5 litres (48 fl oz) red wine, chilled
100 ml (3¹/2 fl oz) dark rum
300 g (10 oz) blanched almonds, toasted

Place the Vermouth, Fernet-Branca, raisins, orange rind, cardamom, cloves, ginger, cinnamon sticks and sugar in a saucepan and bring to the boil over medium heat. Reduce the heat to low and simmer for 10 minutes. Remove and allow to cool. Add the chilled wine, dark rum and toasted almonds, and pour into a punch bowl or large jug. Serves 15–20.
note – Chilled knight may be served cold as a spicy late-night summer's drink, or warmed as a mulled wine on a winter's night.

chilled knight

eccles cakes

30 g (1 oz) dried peaches, choped
30 g (1 oz) currants
1/4 teaspoon ground nutmeg
1/4 teaspoon ground allspice
1/4 teaspoon ground cinnamon
1 teaspoon caster (superfine) sugar
2 tablespoons orange juice
1 teaspoon finely chopped orange zest
2 teaspoons finely chopped lemon zest
2 sheets ready-prepared puff pastry, thawed
milk, to glaze
icing (confectioners') sugar, for dusting

Place all the ingredients except the pastry and milk in a bowl and mix well. Stamp out ten rounds of pastry using an 8 cm (3 inch) cookie cutter. Place 1 teaspoon of the fruit mix to one side of each pastry round and fold over to form a half moon. Press the edges together with a fork or your fingers. With a sharp knife, make a couple of slits in the top of each pastry. Place on a baking tray lined with baking paper and brush the tops with a little milk to glaze. Bake for 12–15 minutes, or until golden brown. Remove and lightly dust with icing sugar. Makes 10.

ginger hearts

2 cups plain (all-purpose) flour
1 teaspoon baking powder
3 teaspoons ground ginger
1 teaspoon ground cinnamon
pinch ground cloves
85 g (3 oz) unsalted butter, softened
1/2 cup dark brown sugar
1 egg
1 tablespoon molasses*
1/4 cup raw sugar crystals

Preheat the oven to 180°C (350°F). Sift the flour and spices into a bowl. In another bowl, cream the butter and brown sugar until light and fluffy, and add the egg, beating well. Stir through the molasses. Fold this mixture through the sifted dry ingredients until combined. Gather into a ball. Roll out the dough between two sheets of baking paper to a thickness of 5 mm (1/4 inch). Cut heart shapes from the dough with a 5 cm (2 inch) cookie cutter and sprinkle evenly with raw sugar crystals. Transfer to a baking tray and bake for 12 minutes. Cool on a wire rack. Makes 36.

chocolate truffles

125 g (4 oz) dark chocolate
50 g (1 3/4 oz) sour cream
2 teaspoons finely grated orange rind
1/8 teaspoon ground cardamom
1/4 cup unsweetened cocoa powder

Place the chocolate in a bowl over a saucepan of simmering water. When the chocolate has melted, fold in the sour cream, orange rind and cardamom. Stir well, then place in the refrigerator for 30 minutes or until set.
Place the cocoa powder in a shallow bowl. Drop a teaspoon at a time of the chocolate mixture into the cocoa. Toss to cover the chocolate with the cocoa, then roll the chocolate into a ball in the palm of your hand, covering the outside with more cocoa. When all the truffles have been rolled, place them in an airtight container in the refrigerator until ready to serve. Makes 25.

chocolate brownies

125 g (4 oz) unsalted butter
125 g (4 oz) dark chocolate
4 eggs
300 g (10 oz) caster (superfine) sugar
1 cup plain (all-purpose) flour
1/4 cup Dutch cocoa powder
1 teaspoon vanilla essence
60 g (2 oz) roughly ground hazelnuts
icing (confectioners') sugar or unsweetened
  cocoa, to serve

Preheat the oven to 180°C (350°F). Melt the butter and chocolate in a medium-sized saucepan over low heat, stirring occasionally, until smooth. Allow to cool for 10 minutes. Beat the eggs and sugar in a large bowl until light and fluffy, then gradually add the cooled chocolate mix. Fold in the flour, cocoa powder, vanilla essence, hazelnuts and a pinch of salt. Pour into a greased 20 x 30 cm (8 x 12 inch) baking tin lined with baking paper and bake for 30 minutes, or until the edges begin to pull away from the baking tin. Allow to cool in the tin. Cut into small squares and dust with icing sugar or unsweetened cocoa to serve. Makes approximately 35 squares.

eccles cakes

chocolate truffles

ginger hearts

chocolate brownies

glossary

asian dried shrimps

Dried shrimps are available from most Asian grocery stores and can be bought either whole or shredded. They are used as a flavouring agent in many stocks, or as an ingredient in relishes and sambals.

bamboo steamer

This inexpensive woven Asian container made from bamboo has a lid and slatted base. Food is placed inside the container and then placed over a saucepan of boiling water to cook. Bamboo steamers are available from Asian grocery stores and most large supermarkets.

black sesame seeds

Mostly used in Asian cooking, black sesame seeds add colour, crunch and a distinct nuttiness to whatever dish they garnish. They can be found in most Asian grocery stores. Purchase regularly, as the seeds can become rancid with age.

bocconcini

These are small balls of mozzarella, often sold in their own whey. When fresh they are soft and springy to the touch and taste distinctly milky. Available from most delicatessens.

brioche dough

50 ml (1³/₄ fl oz) milk
¹/₂ sachet (7 g/¹/₄ oz) dry yeast
2 cups plain (all-purpose) flour
35 g (1¹/₄ oz) caster (superfine) sugar
3 eggs
125 g (4 oz) unsalted butter, softened

Heat the milk in a small saucepan until it is lukewarm. Remove from the heat and pour into the bowl of an electric mixer, along with the yeast and 3 tablespoons of the flour.

Leave covered for 10 minutes to activate the yeast. When the yeast mix is bubbling on the surface, add the remaining flour, sugar, eggs and 1 teaspoon of sea salt, and begin to mix the dough on a low speed. After a few minutes the dough should start to come together. Add the butter slowly and beat on a higher speed until the dough is shiny and elastic. Transfer to a bowl and cover with plastic wrap. Refrigerate for a minimum of 4 hours.

candied zest

Place the zest in a pot of cold water over high heat. As soon as it comes to the boil, remove and drain the water away. Cover with cold water and repeat the process two more times. Place the boiled zest into a simmering pot of sugar syrup* for a couple of minutes, then remove and roll in caster (superfine) sugar. Allow to dry overnight on a bed of sugar.

capers

These are the green buds from a Mediterranean shrub, preserved in a brine solution or in salt. The salted capers have a firmer texture. Rinse away the salt before using them. Available from good delicatessens.

caponata

1 large eggplant (aubergine), cut
  into 1 cm (¹/₂ inch) dice
¹/₄ cup (2 fl oz) olive oil
1 clove garlic, minced
1 red capsicum (pepper), finely diced
1 teaspoon thyme leaves
2 tablespoons tomato paste
1 tablespoon salted capers,
  rinsed and drained
2 tablespoons finely sliced green olives
1 tablespoon finely chopped anchovies
1 cup finely chopped fresh parsley

Lightly salt the eggplant and leave it to drain in a colander for 20 minutes. Rinse and pat dry with paper towels. Heat the oil in a heavy-based saucepan over moderate heat and add the garlic. Stir for a minute, then add the eggplant. Cook, stirring occasionally, until the eggplant is lightly golden, then add the capsicum, thyme, tomato paste and ¹/₂ cup (4 fl oz) of water. Reduce the heat and leave to simmer, covered, for 15 minutes, then add the capers, olives and anchovies. Allow to cool. Before serving, fold in the parsley.

chilli syrup

2 large red chillies
¹/₂ cup sugar

Place the chillies, sugar and ¹/₂ cup (4 fl oz) of water in a small saucepan and bring to the boil. Reduce the heat and simmer for 5 minutes. Remove the chillies, cool the syrup and place in a jar or bottle. Store in the refrigerator until ready to use.

crème fraîche

A mixture of naturally soured cream and fresh cream, crème fraîche is lighter than sour cream. Available from gourmet food stores and some large supermarkets.

crêpe mixture

1 cup plain (all-purpose) flour
4 eggs
1 teaspoon baking powder
50 g (1³/₄ oz) butter, melted
300 ml (9¹/₂ fl oz) milk

Whisk together the flour, eggs, baking powder, butter and a pinch of salt. Slowly add the milk and whisk until smooth. Allow the batter to sit for a few hours, or preferably overnight.

daikon

Daikon, or mooli, is a large white radish. Its flavour varies from mild to quite spicy, depending on the season and variety. Daikon contains an enzyme that aids digestion. It can be freshly grated or slow-cooked in broths, and is available from most large supermarkets or Asian grocery stores. Select firm and shiny vegetables with unscarred skins.

dried asian fried onions

Crisp-fried shallots or onions are available from most Asian grocery stores and are normally packaged in plastic tubs or bags. They are often used as a flavour enhancer, scattered over rice and savoury dishes.

edible silver leaf

Silver leaf, or varak, is flavourless, safe to eat and available from Indian grocery stores. Both gold and silver leaf are also available from cake decorating shops. Both are extremely fragile. Remove the leaf from the paper it is attached to at the last minute by simply turning the paper over and applying the leaf to any surface or liquid.

feta cheese

Feta is a salty, pickled cheese which is maintained in a 'young' state by the brine in which it is immersed. It must be kept in this brine during storage or it will deteriorate quickly. Available from delicatessens and most supermarkets.

filo pastry tart shells

2 ready-prepared filo pastry sheets
50 g (1 3/4 oz) butter, melted
thyme leaves, finely chopped

Preheat the oven to 160°C (315°F). Place the two filo sheets onto a clean, dry cutting board. Cut in half lengthways and place one half on top of the other. Cut in half lengthways again and repeat the process until you have a pile of squares approximately 5 x 7 cm (2 x 2 3/4 inches). Lightly butter two shallow muffin or tartlet trays. Line each of the moulds with one sheet of filo, pressing the pastry well into the sides. Brush with melted butter and scatter some thyme leaves on top. Cover with a second piece of filo pastry, brush with butter and bake for a few minutes until the pastry is lightly golden. Remove and allow to cool. Makes 36.

ginger juice

Fresh ginger juice is produced by finely grating fresh ginger and then squeezing the liquid from the pithy grated flesh. Use ginger juice to flavour dressings and marinades.

ginger, pickled

Japanese pickled ginger is available from most large supermarkets. The thin slivers of young ginger root are pickled in sweet vinegar and turn a distinctive pink colour in the process. The vinegar is an ideal additive to sauces where a sweet, gingery bite is called for.

ginger syrup

1/2 cup grated ginger
1 cup sugar

Place the ginger, sugar and 1/2 cup (4 fl oz) of water in a small saucepan and bring to the boil. Reduce the heat and simmer for 5 minutes. Strain into a container, cool and store in the refrigerator until ready to use.

gravlax

Gravlax is a sugar-cured salmon flavoured with dill. It is available from delicatessens and some supermarkets. Thinly sliced smoked salmon can be used as a substitute.

haloumi cheese

Haloumi is a semi-firm sheep's milk cheese. It has a rubbery texture which becomes soft and chewy when the cheese is grilled or fried. Available from delicatessens and most large supermarkets.

indian lime pickle

See lime pickle

lemon dipping sauce

juice of 2 lemons
2 star anise
3 cardamom pods
1/4 cup sugar
2 teaspoons light soy sauce

Place all the ingredients in a small saucepan and simmer over medium heat for 5 minutes. Allow to cool before serving.

lemon mayonnaise

2 egg yolks
1 lemon, rind grated and juiced
1 cup (8 fl oz) vegetable oil

In a bowl, whisk the egg yolks, grated rind and lemon juice together. Slowly drizzle in the oil, whisking the mixture until it becomes thick and creamy. Season with salt and white pepper.

lime pickle

Lime pickle is available from Indian grocery stores or large supermarkets. It is usually used as a side dish in Indian cooking.

mascarpone

A heavy, Italian-style set cream which is used as a base in many sweet and savoury dishes. Available from good delicatessens and supermarkets.

mirin

Mirin, or sweet cooking sake, is a syrup used to add sweetness to many sauces and dressings, and for marinating and glazing, as in teriyaki. Available from Asian grocery stores and most large supermarkets.

molasses

A thick, brown syrup obtained from sugar during the refining process, molasses is most commonly found in gingerbread and heavy fruitcake recipes. Available from health food stores and large supermarkets.

mozzarella

Fresh mozzarella can be found in most delicatessens and is easily identified by its smooth, white appearance and ball-like shape. Not to be confused with the mass-produced mozzarella, which is mostly used as a pizza topping, it is usually kept in a lightly salted brine or whey.

nori

Nori is an edible seaweed sold in paper-thin sheets. To concentrate the flavour, lightly roast the sheets on the shiny side over a low flame. Nori sheets are available from most large supermarkets, health food shops and Asian grocery stores.

orange flower water

This perfumy distillation of bitter-orange blossoms is used mostly as a flavouring in baked goods and drinks. Available from delicatessens and large supermarkets.

palm sugar

Palm sugar, or jaggery, is obtained from the sap of various palm trees and is sold in rounded cakes or cylinders and plastic jars. It can be found in Asian grocery stores or large supermarkets. Dark brown sugar is a suitable substitute when palm sugar is unavailable.

pancake mixture

1 cup self-raising (self-rising) flour
40 g (1¼ oz) caster (superfine) sugar
1 egg
150 ml (5 fl oz) milk

Place the flour, sugar and ½ teaspoon of salt in a bowl. In a separate bowl, beat the egg and milk together. Pour into the flour mixture and lightly fold together. Allow the batter to rest for 10 minutes before using.

pancetta

Pancetta is the salted belly of pork. It is sold in good delicatessens, especially Italian ones, sometimes rolled and finely sliced but more often in large pieces ready to be diced or roughly cut. Pancetta adds a rich bacon flavour to dishes.

panettone

An aromatic northern Italian yeast bread with raisins and candied peel, panettone is traditionally eaten at Christmas, when it can be found in most Italian delicatessens or large supermarkets in decorative boxes.

pastry cream

50 g (1¾ oz) caster (superfine) sugar
2 egg yolks
25 g (¾ oz) cornflour (cornstarch)
1 vanilla bean
1 cup (8 fl oz) milk
25 g (¾ oz) unsalted butter

Whisk the sugar, egg yolks and cornflour together in a bowl. Split open the vanilla bean and place it in a saucepan with the milk. Slowly bring to the boil, then remove from the heat and whisk ⅓ cup (2¾ fl oz) of the hot milk into the egg mixture. Quickly tip this mixture into the saucepan containing the remainder of the milk, and whisk together. Return the pan to the heat and bring back to the boil, stirring constantly. Boil for 1 minute. Pass through a sieve into a bowl and discard the vanilla bean. Add the butter and stir until melted. Allow the pastry cream to cool. Cover with plastic wrap and keep refrigerated until ready to use.

pesto

Available ready-made in most supermarkets, pesto is a puréed sauce traditionally made from basil, garlic, parmesan, pine nuts and olive oil.

pickled ginger

See ginger, pickled

pizza dough

½ sachet (7 g/¼ oz) dry yeast
1 teaspoon sugar
1½ cups plain (all-purpose) flour
2 tablespoons olive oil

Place the yeast, sugar and ⅔ cup (5½ fl oz) of warm water into a bowl. Mix gently, then leave for 5 minutes until the yeast is active and the surface is bubbling slightly. Place the flour and 1 teaspoon of sea salt into a large bowl and make a well in the centre. Add the olive oil to the yeast mix and pour the liquid into the flour. Work the mixture together with your hands until the dough just comes together. Turn out onto a floured surface and knead for a few minutes, or until the dough is soft and elastic. Place in an oiled bowl, cover with a cloth or plastic wrap and place in a warm place for 1 hour, by which time the dough should have doubled in size. Punch down and place onto a floured surface. Roll out thinly and cut out 24 x 8 cm (3 inch) rounds. Place on a baking tray and leave for a further 30 minutes. Cover with toppings and bake in a preheated 180°C (350°F) oven for 15 minutes. Makes 24 small pizzas.

plum sauce

1 tablespoon Chinese black vinegar
1 tablespoon rice wine
2 tablespoons sugar
1 teaspoon light soy sauce
1 tablespoon vegetable oil
1¹/₂ teaspoons minced garlic
2 teaspoons grated fresh ginger
4 blood plums, skin and stones removed

Place the vinegar, rice wine, sugar, soy sauce and ¹/₂ cup (4 fl oz) of water in a small jug and set to one side. Place the oil in a small saucepan over medium heat. Add the garlic and ginger and fry for 1 minute before adding the plums. Cook until the plums are beginning to disintegrate, then add the liquid ingredients. Simmer for 15 minutes, remove from the heat and cool.

pomegranate molasses

This is a thick syrup made from the reduction of pomegranate juice. It has a bittersweet flavour, which adds a sour bite to many Middle Eastern dishes. Available from Middle Eastern speciality stores, the closest substitute is sweetened tamarind.

pre-baked tart shells
See shortcrust pastry

prosciutto
Prosciutto is lightly salted and air-dried ham. It is most commonly bought in paper-thin slices, and is available from delicatessens and large supermarkets.

pumpernickel
A dark, heavy-textured rye bread leavened with a sourdough culture, pumpernickel can be bought from delicatessens and large supermarkets.

quince paste
Quinces are large, aromatic fruits with a high pectin content. When cooked and reduced, the resulting paste is of a jelly-like consistency and has a rich pink colour. Quince paste can be purchased at most delicatessens.

rice paper
Edible rice paper sheets are available from most large supermarkets or speciality cookware shops. The thin sheets are most commonly used to wrap nougat and panforte.

rosewater
The distilled essence of rose petals, rosewater is used to impart a perfumed flavour to pastries and sweet puddings. It is often used in conjunction with orange flower water, and is available from delicatessens and large supermarkets.

sambal oelek
A hot paste made from pounded chillies, salt and vinegar. Available from Asian grocery stores and most large supermarkets.

shortcrust pastry

200 g (6¹/₂ oz) plain (all-purpose) flour
100 g (3¹/₂ oz) butter

Place the flour, butter and a pinch of salt into a food processor and process for 1 minute. Add 2 tablespoons of iced water and pulse until the mixture comes together. Wrap in plastic wrap and chill for 30 minutes. Roll the pastry out and cut into rounds. Place into greased patty cake or tartlet tins and chill for a further 30 minutes. Prick the bases and fill with rice or baking weights before placing in a preheated 180°C (350°F) oven for 7–10 minutes. Remove and allow to cool. For a sweet pastry, add 1 tablespoon of caster (superfine) sugar or 1 teaspoon of vanilla extract. Makes 36 tart shells.
note – Tart shells that are not used immediately can be stored in the freezer for several weeks. Place in a preheated oven direct from the freezer (it is not necessary to thaw the tart shells first).

silver leaf
See edible silver leaf

somen noodles
These thin, wheat-based Japanese noodles are commonly sold dried and in bundles. Available from Japanese speciality stores, Asian supermarkets and health food stores.

sour cherries and cherry nectar
These bottled, European-style morello cherries are commonly sold in jars, unlike the sweeter tinned dessert cherries. Both the juice and the fruit are used in cooking. Sour cherry nectar is available in tetra packs from most large supermarkets.

stewed rhubarb

300 g (10 oz) rhubarb
  (approximately 7 stems)
1/4 cup caster (superfine) sugar

Trim the rhubarb stems and cut them into four pieces. Place the rhubarb, sugar and 1/4 cup (2 fl oz) of water in a stainless steel saucepan over medium heat. Cover and simmer for 10 minutes. Remove from heat and allow to cool.

sugar syrup

Place 1 cup of sugar in a small saucepan with 1 cup (8 fl oz) of water and bring to the boil, stirring until the sugar dissolves. Cool, then store in a bottle in the refrigerator until ready to use.

sumac

A peppery, sour spice made from dried and ground sumac berries. The fruit of a shrub found in the northern hemisphere, sumac is typically used in Middle Eastern cookery. Available from most large supermarkets and Middle Eastern speciality stores.

tahini

This is a creamy paste made from ground sesame seeds. It is available in jars from most supermarkets.

tamarind water

Tamarind is the sour pulp of an Asian fruit. It is most commonly available compressed in cakes from Asian food stores. To make tamarind water, place 100 g (3 1/2 oz) of tamarind into a bowl and cover with 2 cups (16 fl oz) of boiling water. Allow to steep for 1 hour, stirring occasionally to break up the fibres, then strain. Tamarind concentrates are also available. Blend according to package instructions.

tart shells

See shortcrust pastry

tempura flour

Available in packages from Japanese speciality stores, tempura flour is used to make the light batter used to coat raw food, which is then dipped in hot oil until golden brown.

tortillas

Thin, round, unleavened bread used in Mexican cooking as a wrap or a base for quesadillas (savoury turnovers). Tortillas are available prepackaged in the refrigerator section of most supermarkets.

turkish delight

Turkish delight, or lokum, is a gummy jelly made from sugar syrup and cornflour, and usually flavoured with rosewater or orange flower water. This confectionery, which usually comes dusted with icing sugar, can be purchased from Middle Eastern speciality stores and delicatessens.

vine leaves

These are the large, green leaves of the grapevine, usually found packed in tins, jars or plastic packs in brine, or frozen in batches. They are used in Greek and Middle Eastern cookery to wrap foods for cooking. Vine leaves in brine should be rinsed before using to remove some of the salty flavour. Fresh grape leaves can be simmered in water for 10 minutes or until soft.

waffles

2 cups self-raising (self-rising) flour
2 teaspoons cinnamon
3/4 cup caster (superfine) sugar
75 g (2 1/2 oz) butter, melted
3 eggs, separated
2 1/2 cups (20 fl oz) milk

Sift the flour and cinnamon into a bowl. Add the sugar, mix well and make a well in the centre. In a jug, mix together the melted butter, egg yolks and milk and pour quickly into the flour mixture, whisking to form a smooth batter. In a clean bowl, whisk the egg whites until soft peaks form. Gently fold through the batter. Preheat and lightly grease a waffle iron. Spoon a small amount of the mixture onto the iron, close the lid and cook the waffle until golden. Repeat with the remaining mixture. Makes 16.

wasabi roe

Wasabi roe is available from speciality seafood suppliers. It is the tiny roe of the flying fish, coloured and flavoured with wasabi, a fiery green paste or powder made from the root of the wasabi plant. Wasabi roe is most commonly used as a garnish for the Japanese speciality sushi.

white miso

White miso (actually a pale yellow colour) is the fermented paste of soya beans, salt and either rice or barley. Miso is used extensively in Japanese cooking in soups, dressings, stocks and as an ingredient in sauces and pickles. White miso has a sweet, mellow taste and a relatively low salt content. Available from Asian grocery stores and health food stores.

wonton wrappers

These paper-thin sheets of dough are available either fresh or frozen from Asian grocery stores. They may be wrapped around fillings and steamed, deep-fried or used in broths. The wrappers usually come in both squares and circles and are available in various thicknesses.

conversion chart

1 cup = 250 ml (8 fl oz)
1 Australian tablespoon = 20 ml (4 teaspoons)
1 UK tablespoon = 15 ml (3 teaspoons)
1 teaspoon = 5 ml

CUP CONVERSIONS
1 cup almonds, whole = 155 g (5 oz)
1 cup basil leaves, whole, firmly packed = 50 g (1¾ oz)
1 cup berries, mixed, chopped = 220 g (7 oz)
1 cup cheese, parmesan, finely grated = 100 g (3¼ oz)
1 cup coconut cream = 250 g (8 oz)
1 cup coconut, desiccated = 90 g (3 oz)
1 cup coriander (cilantro) leaves, whole = 30 g (1 oz)
1 cup flour, white = 125 g (4 oz)
1 cup olives, stoned = 155 g (5 oz)
1 cup parsley, flat-leaf (Italian), whole = 20 g (¾ oz)
1 cup raspberries, whole = 125 g (4 oz)
1 cup rice, raw = 220 g (7 oz)
1 cup rocket (arugula) leaves, roughly chopped = 45 g (1½ oz)
1 cup sugar, caster (superfine) = 220 g (7 oz)
1 cup sugar, white = 250 g (8 oz)
1 cup yoghurt, plain = 250 g (8 oz)

LIQUID CONVERSIONS

metric	imperial	US cups
30 ml	1 fl oz	⅛ cup
60 ml	2 fl oz	¼ cup
80 ml	2¾ fl oz	⅓ cup
125 ml	4 fl oz	½ cup
185 ml	6 fl oz	¾ cup
250 ml	8 fl oz	1 cup
375 ml	12 fl oz	1½ cups
500 ml	16 fl oz	2 cups
600 ml	20 fl oz	2½ cups
750 ml	24 fl oz	3 cups
1 litre	32 fl oz	4 cups